WORKING WITH TEACHERS EFFECTIVELY: COMMUNICATION, RELATIONSHIP, AND PROBLEM-SOLVING SKILLS FOR SCHOOL PRINCIPALS

WORKING WITH TEACHERS EFFECTIVELY: COMMUNICATION, RELATIONSHIP, AND PROBLEM–SOLVING SKILLS FOR SCHOOL PRINCIPALS

By

LAWRENCE L. GIANDOMENICO, PH.D.

Associate Professor
Center for Teacher Education
State University of New York
Plattsburgh, New York

and

LAWRENCE SHULMAN, ED.D.

Professor
School of Social Work
Boston University
Boston, Massachusetts

CHARLES C THOMAS • PUBLISHER
Springfield • Illinois • U.S.A.

Published and Distributed Throughout the World by

CHARLES C THOMAS • PUBLISHER
2600 South First Street
Springfield, Illinois 62794-9265

© *1991 by* CHARLES C THOMAS • PUBLISHER

ISBN 0-398-05753-2

Library of Congress Catalog Card Number: 91-21635

With THOMAS BOOKS *careful attention is given to all details of manufacturing
and design. It is the Publisher's desire to present books that are satisfactory as to their
physical qualities and artistic possibilities and appropriate for their particular use.*
THOMAS BOOKS *will be true to those laws of quality that assure a good name
and good will.*

Printed in the United States of America
SC-R-3

Library of Congress Cataloging-in-Publication Data

Giandomenico, Lawrence L.
    Working with teachers effectively : communication, relationship,
and problem-solving skills for school principals / by Lawrence L.
Giandomenico and Lawrence Shulman.
        p.   cm.
    Includes bibliographical references (p.   ) and index.
    ISBN 0-398-05753-2
    1. School supervision—United States.   2. Teacher-principal
relationships—United States.   I. Shulman, Lawrence.   II. Title.
LB2806.4.G52   1991
371.1'06—dc20   91-21635
                                                                      CIP

PREFACE

This book is a practical guide to the communication, relationship, and problem-solving skills that principals and other educational supervisors need to help teachers accomplish meaningful professional growth, solve school-related problems and work together effectively. Written at the application level to deal with real school problems, it presents a practice theory of supervision designed to enable principals to foster professional growth, enrich instructional skills, and maintain positive relationships with individual teachers and the staff as a group. The models are presented to facilitate understanding of both the interactive process and the practice theory of supervision.

This book is equally relevant to all levels and supervisory positions in public schools. The principal is often the focus of many problems which serve as illustrations for the interactive skills but they are applicable to all teacher supervisors. The practice theory suggested includes communication, relationship, and problem-solving skills which were derived from group dynamics and organization theory. The skills are directed at the development of a positive and trusting relationship which utilizes honest and genuine communication. The skills enable principals and teachers to recognize and solve school-related problems while accepting the need and responsibility for their own professional growth. The supervision skills, presented in a variety of school settings, are illustrated with examples of situations which occur often in public education. Interactive skills are presented which enable the supervisors and teachers to accomplish growth as a collaborative endeavor. Goals are developed based on an analysis of contextual considerations rather than personality proclivities of staff members.

The view of practice theory presented in this book suggests specific supervision goals and offers supervisory behaviors that may achieve these goals. Practice situations are offered which enable principals to learn how to implement complex human relations skills associated with the position. For example, in considering the ways in which a newly appointed principal relates to his/her teaching staff, assumptions regarding authority relations are used as a basis for specific supervision goals, thus helping teachers to lower defenses and to communicate openly. Strategies are suggested and likely results are discussed. Productive and unproductive behaviors are presented to illustrate the potential effects more clearly. Other examples deal with understanding the problems of staff resistance in both active and passive forms. The descriptions and examples enable principals to understand why some contacts with teachers go well and others do not.

Organization

The first chapter, which describes an interactive approach to supervision, develops the conceptual foundation, provides an overview of the purposes of supervision, and identifies the functions of the supervisor. There is no treatment of the history and development of supervision as they are treated thoroughly in many other texts. This book is about the process of supervision and focuses on the relationship between the principal and teachers. The major assumptions and the tasks of supervision with teachers are also treated.

The second and third chapters focus on the initial skills needed to begin the supervisory relationship. Time is used as an organizing principle with phases of the supervision process represented by beginning, middle, and end. The importance of a clear working contract with teachers is explained and examples are given to illustrate the skill of contracting. The problems experienced by beginning supervisors from outside the system, as well as inside the system, are discussed and illustrated.

The middle, or work, phase of supervision is explained in Chapters 4 through 7. The core skills involved in all forms of interaction with teachers are defined and illustrated. The importance of genuine empathy, sharing feelings, sharing data, and making a demand for work are among those described and illustrated in these chapters. Resistance in both active and passive forms is explored.

The role of the principal in promoting growth with individual teachers is the focus of Chapter 8. The assumptions which underlie the process of helping a teacher grow are explained. Formal and informal sessions are defined and examples of beginning and experienced teachers are given to illustrate the process skills in the context of each of the different formal sessions. Collecting and analyzing data, planning, and a strategy for conducting productive sessions is explained.

The final chapter is devoted to the supervisor's work with teachers as a staff group. The beginning phase of working with the group lays the foundation for a culture for work. Conducting staff meetings which are both meaningful and productive relies upon a growth-oriented work culture. Facing the issues and discussing them openly is a major part of the culture for work which the principal creates. Dealing with deviant group members is also discussed and examples illustrate common situations which occur in faculty meetings. The supervisor's roles as a source of support and demand are both discussed.

INTRODUCTION

Ten Years as a School Supervisor:
Do I Have to Go to School Tomorrow?

Sept. 1980

G ene, an enthusiastic newly appointed elementary school principal, planned his opening day remarks to staff. Having taught at the school for the past seven years, he felt confident about the transition to administration. He'd been a discontented teacher who was eager to implement changes that he and his colleagues had discussed countless times during teacher room coffee breaks. A recent degree in administration equipped him with a myriad of theoretical constructs so he approached the new year with confidence. After his opening remarks, which focused on an announcement that he planned "to make some changes around here," he began to sense a pall over the room. Peers who had previously been friends seemed to take on a remote stance. His handbook, outlining new schedules and procedures, was met with criticism, and staff began to appear restless/bored. Gene was relieved that the end of the meeting was drawing near but remained perplexed/confused about the atmosphere which he had inadvertently created.

Sept. 1987

Gene, still enthusiastic, has continued to develop his theoretical skills. During the summer he participated in a workshop on Mastery Teaching and felt it was just the thing to introduce to his staff. Despite an investment of countless hours of work and dedication, he still was not satisfied with his supervisory relationship with staff. He was cautiously optimistic that this training program would turn things around for his school. Imagine his frustration when staff resistance to the program caused its abandonment after a few months.

Sept. 1990

Gene, no longer enthusiastic, approached the staff this year at the orientation session with an announcement, "Welcome back to a new school year. Unless there are questions from the floor, you're encouraged to use the rest of the day in preparing your rooms. I know how hectic the openings are for you." Although no overt statements were made, he had some fleeting feelings of guilt that something was missing in his supervisory relationships; but these notions quickly passed when he thought of the pressing issues of the cafeteria schedule, the bussing nightmares of the first week, and the many requests from parents for special assignments for their children.

Where Was I When This Was Covered in Graduate School?

Unfortunately, this set of circumstances, with minor variation, is replicated often across the nation. How can it be that intelligent, well-intentioned, and initially highly motivated individuals have their enthusiasm dulled over time? Given the context of public schools today, principals are truly in a position which is both demanding and difficult. In addition to being on the firing line in countless conflicts and dilemmas created by community, school board, parents, students, and staff issues, principals are expected to lead, indeed engineer change initiatives which may or may not be of their making. Researchers, clear about very little, appear to be of one mind in the view that the principal's role has become more complex, ambiguous, and overburdened during the past twenty years. In a similarly universal vein, researchers express concern that administrators are often ill-prepared for the newly defined expectations created by the "effective schools" findings.

Principals attempting to supervise teachers, may fear that they may not have answers to problems which develop between teachers and children and/or what to do in difficult situations that may arise over disagreements with the teacher. These and other risks, including loss of teacher approval, make the option of not supervising teachers attractive. In some situations, instead of supervision, a tacit agreement is reached which presents the illusion of growth. Both parties engage in the process verbally, but no real expectation exists for action on either part. These circumstances exist at the same time that administrators have been given a national call for leadership at the principal's level. Abandonment of teacher supervision is viewed as counter-productive to the school improvement effort.

Since the publication of *A Nation at Risk* in 1983, direction from various sources for the improvement of public schools has been frequent and varied. Suggestions from private industry, commissions, and research have pointed to the need for and the importance of strong leadership at the building level to insure that the qualities of the school enhance the classroom learning environment. Research from teacher effectiveness suggests that leadership be directed toward insuring that thoroughly planned lessons, focused instruction, and positive classroom discipline measures be present to increase the probability of success for each child. Conclusions from research on school and teacher effectiveness must serve as the goals for the practice of supervision by the building principal. They form the content of supervision practice goals and they are the substance of the desired direction for growth for both the school and individual teacher. Despite frequent calls in the literature and in the media for specific direction for improvement in schools, suggestions on how the school principal is to accomplish these ends are infrequent.

Principals, faced with context difficulties and suggested content directions, must rely on intuition, common sense, and trial and error in order to proceed. Training opportunities do exist for principals, however, and they offer skills in diagnosing and analyzing teaching which helps them in supervision. Similarly, many teachers have attended effective teacher training programs which have made them familiar with the vocabulary and concepts of the technology, but they may be reluctant to apply them in the classroom. They may also require support to help them in their efforts to develop and refine new techniques. Supervision approaches that focus on the technological aspects of growth may be neglecting the most important element in the effort, the individual teacher, and the internal process of growth that is or is not taking place with the teacher. Such efforts frequently result in sessions in which the principal is telling or selling the teacher on what was wrong with a lesson. Teachers, as a result of this, may simply exchange one set of symptoms for another, moving through the technical content of instruction primarily to please the principal. It is not sufficient for the principal to have the technical ability to analyze instruction. He/she must also have the interactive skills necessary to engage the teacher effectively in the process of individual growth.

ACKNOWLEDGMENTS

Heartfelt appreciation is extended to the following graduate students for their help in developing this book: Karl Thelen, Alicia Chase, Cathy Sherman, Richard Kahn, and Jeanette Stapley. Special thanks is also extended to my colleagues: John Madison, Charles Mitchell, Raymond Domenico, and Thomas Moran. I also want to express my gratitude to my family, and especially to my wife, Donna, for her understanding during the project.

L.L.G.

CONTENTS

WORKING WITH TEACHERS EFFECTIVELY: COMMUNICATION, RELATIONSHIP, AND PROBLEM-SOLVING SKILLS FOR SCHOOL PRINCIPALS

Chapter 1

AN INTERACTIONAL APPROACH
TO TEACHER SUPERVISION

For every new principal, the promise of growth and satisfaction achieved through daily work with teachers, students, and parents may be the most powerful source of motivation in taking the job. Professional growth and satisfaction may be sought after goals for many supervisors and principals, but the reality of daily interactions in actual practice, seems to offer more ambiguity than fulfillment.

Floden (1988) reports that schools offer a dichotomy of autonomy and control within an uncertain climate. Teachers may lack power in some respects, but they have almost total control over their own classrooms (Shulman, 1983). Teachers may be thought of as objects of administrative decisions, but it has also been suggested that administrators have little power to bring their behavior into conformity with desired direction (Elmore, 1986), (Weick, 1976). Teachers may close the classroom door to escape culpability for all but the most serious circumstances (Lortie, 1975), (Ross, 1980) and (Sarason, 1971). Floden (1988, 99) refers to the emergent picture as one in which teachers are faced with increasing demands and mandates while feeling oppressed and resisting them. The dilemma is illustrated by Maeroff (1988) who suggests that teachers who have lost the will are not likely to find the way. Schools also present a variety of additional issues which must be dealt with by principals daily.

Even a cursory examination of the main office in most schools will support the conclusion that overseeing a school is no easy task. The high frequency of demands competing for the attention of the principal all seem potentially to affect the routine operation of the school, if left unattended. Fullan (1982, 130) notes that the principal is constantly confronted with conflicts and dilemmas as the role has become more complex, overloaded, and ambiguous over the past twenty years. Fullan also indicates that many administrators who do possess the necessary

3

abilities are likely to report that on-the-job experience contributed the most to their development.

Manasse (1985, 442) summarizes the recent studies on principals' training programs by citing that the preference for verbal communication and concrete information, and the pattern of brief and varied activities, is in stark contrast to the textbooks and teaching style of most graduate programs. Training programs often concentrate on the management aspects of the job (budgeting, time management, report writing, goals/ objectives-setting) and give little attention to the interactional skills required for implementing supervisory and administrative functions. It may be assumed that teachers who do their jobs well should be able to make the transition to supervisory positions on their own. The fact that some teachers become successful administrators may be a tribute to their personality traits and intuition.

There appears to be a need for clear, simple models of proactive supervision that will help school supervisors to understand why some staff contacts go well and others do not (Webster, 1989). There is also a need to implement strategies designed to anticipate and/or ameliorate potential difficulties. Skills in the area of communication, relationship building, teaching adults, and group leadership appear crucial. Blumberg and Jonas (1987, 59) describe the need for these skills and the importance of "psychological acceptance" of the supervisor by the teacher. Research findings are quite conclusive regarding the key role of principals in effective implementation of any school change. Manasse (1985, 453) states "... principals should be a factor in any program legislation, and their importance in the process of setting overall priorities and goals should be recognized."

You Can Understand Practice!

Researchers have been able to tease out competencies which characterize effective supervisors. Among the most frequently identified (Huff, Lake, and Schaalman, 1982) are: (1) commitment to school mission (purpose and direction cluster); (2) concern for image of school, staff, students; (3) participatory management style; (4) tactical adaptability (consensus management cluster); (5) coaching skills; and (6) firmness in enforcing quality standards (quality enhancement cluster). Manasse (1985, 443), in examining the implications of these findings, noted that although many of the competencies were in the cognitive cluster, there were no competencies from this cluster common to all principals. She noted this to be an area where carefully designed training could improve effectiveness. The cognitive competencies identified were monitoring, ability to recognize patterns, perceptual objectivity, and analytical ability. She further hypothesized that these findings suggest that effective principals optimize their many daily interactions by using them to collect information. They are objective in their perceptions and interpretations and are able to see patterns in data collected over a period of time and from a variety of sources. With relatively accurate and complete information, they use their analytic skills to match needs and resources, to weigh conflicting demands and expectations, and to balance priorities. As a result of their analyses, they develop action plans and strategies to implement them. Then, in the course of their daily interactions and informal interchanges around the school, they monitor to see that their plans are moving according to schedule. They apply pressure where appropriate and modify when necessary.

If the above competencies are those most crucial to the success of the effective principal, it appears that changes in current preparation and training are necessary. This book represents a beginning effort to suggest a model of practice that may assist supervisors to develop the analysis skills necessary to recognize, identify and implement plans and strategies for school improvement. The role of the principal and the accompanying skills offered in this book are compatible with the suggested directions learned from past efforts to produce change in schools (Ornstein and Levine, 1990).

Utilizing the practice theory of Schwartz (1961, 1971, 1976, 1977), this chapter describes some of the key ideas of an interactional approach to teacher supervision. The model is constructed so that principals and other school supervisors may learn to isolate the dynamics of interactions and situations which occur commonly and often cause communication to break down. It describes a model for understanding individual teachers as they interact with a number of groups including: students, parents, colleagues, and others involved in the daily operations of schools. The book also provides insight into the supervisor's functional role with respect to that interaction. These concepts are the foundation for the interactional approach to teacher supervision.

The ideas presented in this book represent a form of practice wisdom that has been derived from the experiences of practicing school administrators and they are tentative and constantly evolving. While most of the examples used are drawn from school settings, some have been taken from other environments and modified for use in this book. These illustrate issues which the authors believe are generic for all managers. In analyzing the examples contained in this book, the authors have employed the framework and major elements developed by Schwartz (1962) and elaborated by Shulman (1982). The framework has been adapted and applied to teacher supervision. A number of constructs from social and behavioral science are included in this work and they are not intended as dogma but rather as tools to help the practicing principal and other school supervisors understand the dynamics of teacher supervision.

Underlying Assumptions

Several assumptions underlie the presentation of concepts in this work. First is the belief that there are a number of common dynamic and core skills central to all supervision processes. Second is the belief that the core dynamics and skills which underlie effective supervision can be related to the many different contexts within which school supervisors operate. Many key skills, for example, are equally relevant for working with staff members individually or in groups at the elementary, middle, or secondary school levels.

The third assumption is that there are similarities in the processes that take place in the supervisory relationship and in any teaching encounter. The central dynamics and key skills that are important in teaching are also important in the supervisory relationship. Much of what we know about effective teaching can be useful in implementing diverse aspects of supervision. The final assumption is that there is a parallel process within a school system in which the way a principal relates to the teaching staff may influence the manner in which teachers relate to students, parents, and even colleagues. This assumption views the principal as modeling what she/he believes about helping relationships. In a sense, a principal is teaching all the time with more being "caught" by his/her staff than "taught" by the principal.

Terminology

Practice Theory

This book suggests a practice theory of supervision for principals and other school supervisors. The theory is directed primarily at the effort to foster professional growth, enrich teaching skills, and maintain positive relationships in the supervision of individual teachers and of the building staff as a group. Schwartz (1962, 270) defined practice theory as a system of concepts integrating three conceptual subsystems: one which organizes relevant aspects of social reality; one which conceptualizes specific values and goals; and one which deals with the formulation of interrelated principals of action. These three conceptual subsystems are presented in this book in the following perspectives: context, content, and process. They provide frames of reference from which the elements included in the suggested practice theory are drawn and analyzed.

Context, the first perspective, seeks to explain the social reality of the school environment. It focuses upon the associations and relations of teachers, including both individual and group norms. Content, the second perspective, refers to conceptualized direction such as policy, goals, objectives, procedures, curricula, or other such directives. The third conceptual perspective is process and represents interrelated principles of action drawn from the first two. This chapter uses these perspectives to explain the central ideas of the practice theory suggested.

The practice theory presented here seeks to enable principals identify underlying assumptions derived from knowledge about human behavior and social organization (context). The supervisor learns to identify supervision practice goals (content) based on these assumptions and implement supervisory (process) skills and strategies that may achieve these goals.

Accordingly, this book adapts this model for the school administrator. Drawing on such sources as group dynamics and social psychology theory, an attempt has been made to identify what is known about supervisory relationships. For example, in examining the way a new principal begins to relate to the teaching staff, it is necessary to understand the principles which guide people's behavior in new situations (the effect of role and the impact of authority may be explored). Based on the assumptions drawn from this examination, specific goals for the beginning phase of supervision are suggested, and the skills designed to achieve these goals are identified. For further illustration: what is known about organizational theory and the process of change would provide the basis for examining the dynamics involved in implementing a system-wide curriculum change. Using this knowledge, the principal would incorporate specific goals for a staff meeting designed to lower defenses and to encourage communication. The skills needed to accomplish these goals would be identified.

This book presents a model designed to help supervisors and principals analyze the underlying dynamics of day-to-day problems by systematically identifying: (a) what is known, (b) what is the intent (goal), and (c) the skills that are required.

The purpose of this book is to provide a practical approach which will assist principals and other school supervisors to solve daily problems. Its major value for today's school principal is that it provides a framework for action, not just analysis. In addition, the practice theory may be of significant value in the effort to foster professional growth, enrich teaching skills, and maintain positive relationships in the work of the principal with individual teachers and the building staff as a group.

Model and Skill

The term *model* is used to explain a particular representation of reality. Models are helpful to simplify the complexities of the supervision process. For example, models will be used to describe the relationship between a principal and teacher, the culture of a staff group, the organizational dynamics of the school setting, and the process through which the principal impacts staff. The term *skill* describes behaviors used by supervisors in the execution of their professional functions. For the purposes of this book, the skill foci is directed toward the context of supervision and management. Among the pertinent skills used are relationship, communication, and problem solving.

Task Definition

Alfonso (1986, 2), in discussing the role of supervision, acknowledges that while scholars of supervision differ regarding the process, most would tend to agree that it is related to goal achievement in schools and most directly to the improvement of instruction. An essential element in the supervisor's work in all organizations is his or her direct and continuing relationship with those responsible for production of goods or services. Kadushin (1976) provides a definition of supervision which views a supervisor as having the authority to direct, coordinate, enhance, and evaluate on-the-job performance of the supervisees for whose work he/she is held accountable. In implementing this responsibility, the supervisor performs administrative, educational, and supportive functions with the supervisee in the context of a positive relationship.

This decade has marked consistent reference to the importance of the leadership role of the principal in developing and supervising an effective school. Qualities or characteristics of effective school principals have included reference to a variety of items such as clear goals, order and discipline, and high expectations. These qualities or characteristics are understandable from the content perspective, but they offer little advice to the practicing or aspiring principal as to how (process) such characteristics are to be accomplished. A theme which seems to be ubiquitous as a possible alternative is teacher empowerment. Involvement or participation in decision-making is viewed as a means of increasing a teacher's investment in school development. How this notion and the leadership role of the principal are integrated is left largely unexplored. Proponents of a recently advanced notion view called, situated cognition, argue for a contextualized view of learning through collaborative social interaction (Brown, Collins, & Duguid, 1989). This notion may offer a useful framework to build an effective interactive supervision model for principals.

However, as most supervisors soon find out, the process of carrying out the administrative, educational, and supportive aspects of the job is complicated by the inherent necessity of involving staff along the way. Schwartz indicates that organizing human beings into harmonious and effective work groups is dependent on the ability of the workers to lend themselves wholeheartedly to their task. Shulman (1983, 492) notes that the question is not how central authorities can control teachers or how teachers can be allowed to do their own thing, but how policies can be mandated in a manner likely to enlist the willing cooperation of the teachers as collaborating allies rather than as unwilling subordinates grudgingly conceding their lack of power.

Gronn (1983), in research focusing on the interactive behavior of principals indicates that two-thirds to three-fourths of the principal's total working time is spent talking. Interactive skills are called for in the large amount of time typically given to communication in the daily behavior of most principals. It appears that the ability of the principal to direct teacher behavior must be worked at linguistically (Hodgkinson, 1978, 81). Getting agreement on the direction to be pursued for growth and putting the agreement into practice are two of the most important and significant tasks of supervision. Communication skills are at the center of these tasks. A crucial aspect of teacher supervision is the emphasis on carrying out tasks in interaction with the supervisee within the context of a positive relationship. Without active teacher involvement supervisors are unable to implement their functions effectively.

Principals must develop positive working relationships with teachers and they must be aware of the myriad of barriers that block communication in any given circumstance. The elements which make up a good working relationship can be described as *trust* and *caring*. Teachers need to trust that they can be honest with their principal and that they are able to share what they really think and feel, rather than what they think she/he wants to hear. Trust also means that teachers feel free to share their mistakes and failures with their principal as well as their successes. The caring dimension of the working relationship is related to the belief on the part of the teaching staff that the principal is genuinely concerned about them as professionals, in their own right, not just viewing them as instruments to provide instructional services to students. Until the relational and communication functions of supervision are understood and acknowledged by principals, teacher growth and change may occur fortuitously.

The primary goal of this book is to offer new ways of viewing situations which principals and other school supervisors have reported as difficult for them. The practice theory suggested here offers an alternative intended to apply directly to the current problems of the typical school principal. The emphasis in this book is on interaction with a specific focus on communication, relationship, and problem-solving skills of school principals and supervisors. As a first step, a model for conceptualizing teacher-system relationships relevant to the school supervisor's functional role in these interactions is explained in the following section.

Teacher—Group Interaction

The school principal's view of the supervision process is necessarily influenced by his/her perception of the teachers with whom he/she works. A useful model of supervision conceptualizes teachers as constantly interacting with a number of groups that are related to the work of teaching. A typical public school teacher must deal with a number of groups including children, parents, colleagues, school supervisors, and clerical staff. These relationships are shown in Figure 1.1.

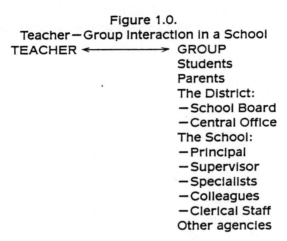

Figure 1.0.
Teacher—Group Interaction In a School
TEACHER ←————————→ GROUP
Students
Parents
The District:
—School Board
—Central Office
The School:
—Principal
—Supervisor
—Specialists
—Colleagues
—Clerical Staff
Other agencies

At any time, teachers could be called up to interact with one or more of these groups. The relationship with each group places unique demands on the teacher and requires specific knowledge and skills if the teacher is to negotiate it effectively.

Effective teaching requires that the professional educator understand the learning process, develop relationships, and apply communications skills with students. In addition, the teacher's knowledge of the problems facing specific students, of the research associated with learner outcomes, of the subject matter, of the curriculum and of the related services available to students will affect the success of his/her work. Many of the communication and relationship skills that are important to the student are also important in dealing with various groups.

The teacher's relationship to the school can be considered from a number of perspectives. First, there are the aspects of job management in which the teacher must be able to work within the structure of the school in terms of time: being on time for work/meetings, meeting deadlines, and organizing/scheduling of classes for effective management of student groups. A second important area is the teacher's ability to relate effectively to policy/procedures. Teachers must implement policies and follow procedures while they are developing the skills necessary to influence them. Also required are skills necessary to deal professionally with colleagues, support staff, and administrators. Teachers need to coordinate their efforts with those of other staff members. When breakdowns occur in faculty relationships, the outcome may affect teaching effectiveness. In addition, teachers must work with supervisors who are symbols of authority, and learn to use this relationship to their advantage.

Obviously, the groups or the systems facing a teacher are complicated. All are not operating simultaneously and some are less urgent than others. By viewing the teacher's function as dynamic and interacting with various groups, the principal can begin the process of partializing tasks and developing an agenda with specific teachers or the staff as a whole. Such an approach affords the opportunity to avoid centering the problems and issues of individuals, thus permitting the focus to be placed on the teacher's activities. It may be better for the principal to deal with the ways teachers may relate effectively to the various groups in the school, for example, than to try to help with a teacher's "problems with authority." The approach of analyzing the teacher's personality, which may be rooted in some early misconceptions, may lead to resistance and complaints by teachers.

Obstacles to Teacher—Group Interactions

Interactions between teachers and individuals representing groups or systems with which they deal don't always go well. It is because of the numerous difficulties that may occur that a supervision function is necessitated. Obstacles emerge from a number of sources. The very complexity of the instructional process may lead to difficulties. Schools are complex and it is easy for teachers to feel overwhelmed by the bureaucracy. Other teachers may be a source of the difficulty or the students, or both. Supervisors may lose track of the realities of the teacher's experiences.

Inaccurate communication is a major source of difficulty in a work situation. Misinterpretations based on stereotypes that teachers and students and administrators hold about one another is a common problem.

Some subjects such as authority and dependency are taboo in our society. The norms which govern communication between peers are powerful. Because of general injunctions against confrontation, normal work-related strains may never be overtly expressed.

Another area which may be a problem in interaction results from the difficulty the staff may have in understanding and acting on the common ground they hold with other groups. Principals depend on staff to carry out their own tasks. Teachers need supervisors who are knowledgeable, supportive, and whose expectations will help them to undertake their work. All school staff members require collegial support.

Such mutual dependence sets the stage for potential obstacles. There are some areas where the needs of the staff and the needs of the administration may not overlap or, in fact, they may be clearly divergent. It is easy to understand why teachers would prefer to have very small classes but political/economic realities of the school may make achieving them impossible.

A conceptualization of the staff in interaction with other groups and the inherent problems will serve as the basis of analysis. This model enables one to identify the people or systems that are involved in the interaction as a tool in theorizing about supervision practice. The identification of obstacles, some of which may be expected, establishes the supervisory function.

The Supervision Process

The definition of the term *supervision* to encompass tasks of administration, education, and support, is helpful for function clarification. However, it lacks practical clarity and it is too general to assist in staff/system interaction analysis. For example, what is the functional role of the principal caught in the middle between angry staff and a superintendent who wants a policy implemented? Both the staff and the superintendent expect the principal to identify with them. The principal may experience pressure from both sides to answer the question: "which side are you on?"

While no one supervisory function can hold true for all cases, it would be helpful if a statement of function could be developed which is applicable to many of the circumstances encountered by the supervisor. If the statement were activity-oriented (what he/she actually does), it could provide a framework for translating difficult situations into more workable units and for developing strategies.

A third force or mediator role can be added now to the interactional model:

To the two elements in the model of a teacher dealing with the various groups shown earlier, the figure above adds a third element, the principal. For the purposes of functional supervision, the principal may be viewed

Figure 1.1.
The Mediation Function of the School Supervisor

TEACHERS ⟵———— (PRINCIPAL) ————⟶ GROUPS

as mediating the interactions of the teacher and the groups with whom he/she interacts. The model suggests that the principal helps the teacher to successfully interact with a variety of groups, utilizing a number of communication, relationship, and problem-solving skills which are presented in the following chapters of this book. For example, in the case of a teacher-parent conflict, the principal might help the two parties talk and listen to each other and discuss differences without losing sight of their common interest. The powerful aspect of this model is that it is functional in a variety of contexts. A principal, having analyzed the factors associated with employment of a new teacher, would have a robust agenda prepared to assist in the adjustment process. Negative and positive aspects are always addressed and often such preparation wards off countless hours of resistance and reactive decision making. In this situation a principal would have anticipated the probable anxiety associated with a new teacher and have helped the staff member to acknowledge apprehensions while also assisting him/her to plan accordingly.

In other situations, when points of conflict between staff and central office personnel arise, a mediative function may include an advocacy role and elements of facilitative confrontation. However, the principal still accepts responsibility for bringing staff issues out in the open that may otherwise lie under the surface and for representing the administration. This process helps to avoid contradictions about allegiances, promotes honest confrontation, and permits neutrality where appropriate. Obviously, there are also functional responsibilities required of principals in addition to those subsumed under the mediation concept. The need to terminate a nonproductive employee is one example.

Generally, however, the function of mediator may prove to be a powerful tool in the conceptual framework. The principal will be able to optimize his/her daily interactions by using the data gathered through observation. By identifying the issues, likely to be in operation, as staff members perform their various tasks, the principal uses interactive skills to assist, confront, or educate as needed. This type of interaction would continue throughout the day both formally and informally.

In all situations the most important aspect of the practice theory is the interactional nature of the process. Both teachers and the principal are dependent upon each other for active involvement. Those who collaborate in the process find that it promotes trust, commitment, and learning on all sides.

Chapter 2

BUILDING AN EFFECTIVE
RELATIONSHIP WITH TEACHERS:
PREPARATORY AND BEGINNING SKILLS

The beginning phase of the principal's work with teachers is critical to the successful establishment of an effective relationship. It is extremely important for both the principal and the teachers to be well prepared to make a good start of the supervisory relationship. The initial meeting or encounter may set the tone and expectations for future interaction. Pressing issues which are part of the immediate experience of the faculty may foster reactions if no mention is made of them. Issues which are ignored or not dealt with appropriately may result in closing the supervisory relationship before it has a chance to develop. These issues may remain beneath the surface continuing to affect the relationship for months and even years.

The problem of a good start with teachers is made all the more difficult by the fact that both principal and staff are inexperienced with each other and tension and uncertainty may be high. Preparatory work, understanding the dynamics associated with new relationships, knowledge about the use of core skills, and some teacher-specific information can facilitate the process. In the following section, the skills and processes associated with preparing for and beginning a supervisory relationship will be explored.

Figure 2.0 outlines some of the major factors which inhibit the development/sustenance of relationships between supervisors and teachers. While some of the factors may appear simplistic, often they are the barriers which undermine well-intentioned, and otherwise well planned change and growth initiatives. This chapter will expand on the contextual factors which help create the obstacles to effective relationship-building and provide supervisors with action strategies which will mitigate their effects. It is the author's intent to train supervisors to analyze the probable impact of these phenomena whenever an interaction appears to be breaking down or is stalled. In addition, proactive and preparatory strategies will be outlined.

Relationship Modeling

The interactive skills used by the principal or school supervisor are applicable to the relationship of teachers with children. Teachers may draw upon the skills demonstrated by the principal as a model for solving problems with children. Appropriate modeling by the principal is a positive by-product or effect of the techniques suggested here. An open trusting relationship cultivated by the principal or supervisor with teachers, provides support for effective relationships between teachers and children in the classroom.

Phases of Supervision Work with Teachers

For purposes of clarity, the supervision work of the principal is organized chronologically. The phases of supervision are: (1) preliminary; (2) beginning; (3) middle, also referred to as the work phase; and (4) ending and transition. The four phases are relevant to all the interactions of supervisors with teachers. The most frequent areas of interaction in the examples used here are the staff meeting and the supervision conference, but the skills are useful in guiding the supervisor's behavior in even the most brief encounters with teachers. The middle phase of supervision (see Chapters 4–7), where skills are most penetrating, are described as conference skills.

The Preliminary Phase: Tuning In

As suggested earlier, the beginning of the supervision relationship with teachers is important. This process involves two steps which are not required to be in order. Before the initial meeting with the staff as a group and individual interactions with faculty, the new principal or supervisor must engage in personal preparation for that interaction. The first effort in the preliminary phase of teacher supervision is preparatory empathy, referred to by Shulman (1982) as tuning in. The principal must tune in to his/her own feelings regarding the interaction. A second and equally important area is considering the feelings of the teachers. The objective is to put oneself in the place of the other to feel, as closely as possible, the problems, issues, and needs that may be present but not easily communicated.

The Importance of Indirect Communication

In supervisory relationships, indirect communication is often used as a means of avoiding potential negative consequences. The freedom to engage in direct criticism must be developed in the relationship. Trust and respect must be the foundation on which such communication takes place. Tuning in helps the principal to anticipate and look for subtle cues couched in indirect communication. This enables the principal to use such circumstances as an opportunity to demonstrate supportive behaviors which develop trust and build the foundation for an effective relationship with teachers.

An Example of Tuning-In: The New Middle School Principal

The experience of Judy, a new middle school principal, provides an illustration of how tuning-in works. Judy was an extremely well-regarded third-grade teacher for twelve years before being appointed to the position of middle school principal. During the first staff meeting, one of the eighth grade teachers asked her if she had recent experience working with emerging adolescents, whose behavior may be both extremely active and unpredictable. Judy found herself both uncomfortable and unprepared for such a challenge. She felt she had been put on the spot in the very area about which she herself was concerned. In her reply to the teacher, Judy said that she had adolescent children of her own, she had worked with church groups of that age, and she had taken graduate courses which included the study of such children and, as such, she felt adequately equipped to deal with the situation.

During a follow-up peer supervision meeting, Judy brought up the issue and the group discussed the implications of her responses. She recognized her response as mildly defensive and in retrospect agreed it was precipitated by her own anxiety about preparedness for the position. The group conjectured that Judy's response may begin to build a wall which acts as a barrier to genuine communication with her staff. Her actions were, however, very understandable for an anxious new principal. Judy could have tuned-in to her own insecurities and recognized her fears and doubts for what they were. She could have also tuned-in to the concerns that the teachers may have, such as whether a person with lower elementary experience is able to cope with older kids who tend to act out much more. Possibly they worried that when they sent disruptive students to the office she would view them too softly and undermine the strong discipline code they needed to teach effectively in a middle school.

Given such circumstances, the question, "Have you had recent experience with emerging adolescents?" may not have been an attack on Judy's competence but an indirect way of raising an important concern. A principal who was tuned-in to the possible meaning of this comment could have avoided making a defensive response. Instead, a skill defined by Schwartz (1976) as responding directly to an indirect cue, could be used effectively in this situation to help build mutual trust and respect. The exact form of this skill would vary according to the personality and style of the principal. One example might be to say: "No, I have not had much experience in dealing with emerging adolescents in the school setting. Frankly, I am concerned about that. I wonder if you are concerned that I might not understand what it's like to teach such children, how difficult and disruptive they can be, and how important it would be for me to take a firm stand in support of enforcement of the discipline code. I will rely on your judgment and suggestions as I develop a better understanding of such children in the coming months."

In this response the effort is to respond directly to an indirect cue. Such a response is more likely to be viewed by staff as an honest expression of concern. It also leaves room for the staff to develop the desired response by the principal to disruptive students sent to the office. Such honesty could begin to open the supervisory relationship or, at the very least, avoid closing off discussion in difficult areas where the competence of the principal is questioned. The staff would not be as likely to regard this response as defensive. The risking and expression of vulnerability by the principal would also model the skills teachers need to develop, for example, in dealing with parents who inquire: "do you have any children?"

Some Cautions About Tuning-In

The new principal may find it difficult to tune-in to the feelings of teachers, particularly in areas where his/her own feelings are uncertain. Beginning under the pressure of thinking the leader must show no weakness and give perfect answers to all questions, may be a fundamental error. Often the new principal is thrust into the new job with little thought given to the type of preparation suggested here. Attempting to appear composed and all-knowing may be giving teachers the message that no help and support is necessary. If uncertainties are withheld and important issues are not attended to appropriately, the very image the new principal was trying to avoid may be projected. The discomfort faced in such situations by the principal and the teachers can be dealt with, as a later example will illustrate.

The preliminary effort to consider the feelings of teachers can also be misdirected, thus providing the principal with false information. Consider the new principal who was promoted over a popular person from inside the school district. The principal tunes in to what *he thinks* will be discontent at the first sign of an indirect cue, and says, "I recognize your anger over my selection instead of Joe." The teachers stare at him with a blank look and say "No, we are not upset about you." The principal replies "Look, I can understand that you would have supportive feelings for Joe." Another teacher quickly assures him that it is not an issue, but the principal stubbornly persists, insisting that the staff must be upset with him. Finally one teacher says, "This discussion really is making me mad!"

It is important to recognize that tuning-in is not an absolutely infallible means of tapping into teachers' feelings and concerns. The principal or supervisor must remain flexible and ready to focus upon the reality of the circumstances. A problem which must be avoided is projecting feelings which do not really concern teachers at that time. The process is not as subtle as it may appear. The principal must be careful not to keep reaching for feelings that are not there. In areas where he/she is fairly certain that concerns are present, a second attempt to reach for them may be made but care must be taken not to push emotion on the teachers. "I know all of you like Joe, and it would not surprise me if you were disappointed that he did not get the position." The message behind this second reach for feelings is that it's all right to discuss sensitive matters such as these. This second attempt to reach for feelings avoids an accusation and teachers may now, or at some later time, feel free to discuss the issue. If teachers do not take up a second offer, the supervisor must drop it.

Although tuning-in and responding directly to indirect cues are presented within the context of examples of newly appointed principals, they are useful in all supervisory situations with teachers when open, honest communication is needed. They are particularly relevant in the preliminary and beginning phases of supervision work with teachers because impressions may be created by what is not done as well as what is accomplished. These impressions may help to develop an open, honest relationship or they may have the effect of erecting a wall which closes discussion and negatively affects the relationship.

Implementation of the skills of tuning-in and responding directly to indirect cues is not easy on a daily basis. In reality, job stress and the pace of the work may often result in the principal missing many of the faculty's indirect cues. There are no paragons of virtue who are always tuned in and receptive. Effective supervision, as defined in this book, involves catching one's mistakes as quickly as possible. A principal who did respond to cues in the first months on the job can always go back and reopen issues. A principal who misses the underlying issues only hinted at by the faculty during a meeting can return to them at future meetings. A highly skilled principal is defined in this book as one who catches his/her mistakes during the same encounter in which they are made.

A legitimate question often raised by principals in workshops is "Who tunes in to me?" This is a reflection of the parallel process in which a principal needs to find sources of support for her or himself in order to be able to provide it for the teaching staff. A principal who is under constant pressure from a nonsupportive superintendent will have a more difficult time in being emotionally available to the faculty. Fortunately, other sources of social support may be found from peers and even one's own faculty. Thus change can start at any level in a school system and a principal does not need to wait for it to begin at the top.

Discussion of "Under the Surface" Issues

Tuning-in offers advantages to school supervisors in dealing with many issues. Take the introduction of a new policy by the central office as an example. Tuning in to teachers' concerns about such a policy and how it will likely affect them may provide the principal with the opportunity to develop responses to indirect cues that help to open discussion and avoid subsequent trouble. When teachers' reactions to such circumstances are kept below the surface, honest communication becomes less likely. The accumulation of such feelings under the surface of regular communication channels encourages discontent and fosters poor cooperation between the supervisor and his/her staff. Planning to reach for such feelings and being ready to discuss them, helps avoid defensive comments which may make teachers view the principal as aggressive and unwilling to discuss difficult subjects. Principals must ask themselves if they are ready for such open communication, and they must be prepared to modify their own behavior accordingly to match the level of honesty and trust which they are asking for from their teachers. Once again, the availability of social support for the principal may be a crucial factor in determining such readiness.

Working with Teachers: The Beginning Phase

Teachers, anticipating the appearance of the new principal, frequently discuss what kind of person he/she will be. Often they will talk about the qualities of their former principal in both good and poor terms as speculation ensues. Of particular interest will be the supervisor's use of authority and what impact his or her style will have on established routines and school rituals. They may wonder how the principal will view the purpose of supervision and what role he/she will carve out for him/herself. These concerns about the authority of the principal will surely be there when the first staff meeting is held. Teachers may not bring them up or commit them to words but they will be there under the surface. Planning to reach for the concerns of teachers, particularly honest expressions of negative feelings, is far better than letting them grow under the surface.

Teachers will be most interested in the role the new principal will play in the supervision of classroom teaching. What issues will be the focus of his/her concern in teaching children? Will there be a new conference format for postobservation discussions? Will written evaluations be formal and specific? How often will the new principal observe teaching and visit classrooms? The role and the purposes that the new principal brings with his/her individual view of supervision involve issues of how authority will be used and what effects will ensue for teachers.

The building principal is a powerful figure in the daily life of classroom teachers. Past experiences are also an issue which affects views of the staff and the principal. Tension is always a part of such new supervision relationships until many of the questions are answered. Teachers draw conclusions from the absence of discussion on such questions when few opportunities for direct conversation are presented. This situation may result in an extended period of testing in which teachers try to figure out what the principal is going to do. Lack of certainty on issues as important as these may cause great anxiety for teachers and a poor supervision relationship for the principal when both are unnecessary.

The questions of supervisory role, purpose, and authority are crucial issues that will greatly affect the relationship between the principal and the teaching staff. Contracting (Shulman, 1982) is a process which may be used by the principal to achieve a mutual understanding with teachers which provides structure and freedom in the supervision relationship. This process may provide answers to issues before they become haunting questions. It seeks to eliminate the hidden agenda items which permit negative feelings and emotions to block a climate of mutual trust and cooperation before they are formed. The following section considers some of the reasons why many critical issues in supervision are seldom raised directly by teachers and often avoided by principals. The specific skills that will help the principal to resolve these important issues are described and illustrated with examples.

Using Contracting Skills to Work with Teachers

There are at least four fundamental skills of contracting in the beginning phase of teacher supervision. These call for the principal to share his/her sense of the purpose of supervision, to explore the supervisory role, to reach for staff feedback on their perceptions, and to discuss the mutual obligations and expectations related to supervisory authority. While this process may appear to be straightforward in theory, it is quite complex in practice.

When principals are asked to explain their role and the kind of assistance they offer to new teachers, often there is a period of silence followed by a question such as "what kind of assistance is needed?" When this question is answered by a further query on the type of help available, an ambiguous, global, or jargon type answer may follow such as "facilitate growth," or "improve your teaching."

Simple phrases may not lend themselves to a description of the role of the principal in teacher supervision, especially when it is not clearly defined or understood by the incumbent. It has been suggested (Joyce, 1983) that a tacit agreement often exists between teachers and principals in which both agree not to intrude on the other. This agreement represents a norm in schools and informal sanctions in the form of social pressures are often used by teachers on principals to induce compliance. It appears that in many cases teachers prefer not to be supervised.

Issues of authority in schools are seldom confronted directly. The preferred means of dealing with such sensitive matters is usually through indirect communication or informal discussion to which the principal is not privy. The new principal wants to be accepted by the teachers and may not risk a discussion on his/her supervisory role which may result in him being viewed as aggressive or authoritative. Another source of uncertainty regarding the role of the principal in teacher supervision may be the central office supervisor. If the principal is given mixed messages about direction in the role, he/she may not truly know what the expectations for his/her role may be. Such ambiguity can lead to hesitancy and reluctance for direct discussion about the purpose, role, and function of supervision with teachers. As such, both teachers and the principal have reasons for not clarifying authority issues.

The Principal's Role as Teacher and Learner

Some principals may fear being asked to deliver if they offer specific assistance in direct discussions of their role in supervision. An example of such a contracting statement could be, "I will observe your class and we will discuss strategies for helping students having the most difficulty." Principals may be concerned that teachers may ask questions and seek assistance that they cannot provide. This fear stems from the idea that the principal must have the perfect answer to all questions because he/she is the instructional leader. Such a belief fails to recognize the value of the principal's role in supervision as both teacher and learner.

Albeit the above reasons explain why the supervision relationship with teachers is allowed to remain vague, the price for such neglect is hardly worth the cost. Such a lack of clarity in the role allows stereotyped images and past experiences to dominate the view teachers have of what may be the best intentions of the principal to develop harmonious relationships. Clearly an alternative to this unintended consequence is necessary. The following example suggests one alternative.

An Example of Contracting: John, New Principal of Millard School

Considerable variation in the way contracting takes place is accounted for by the particular aspects of the district, the school, the staff, and the personality of the principal. All of these issues have implications for the specific content of the contract. In the following example, John, a newly appointed elementary principal, explained his efforts and clarified the purpose of supervision, his role, and the issues of authority at an early teachers meeting.

He began by telling them, "It may help us to develop a mutual understanding if I describe my approach to supervision. I want to hear your ideas about my role so your comments are equally important as well. I see my role as a partner to each of you in our work in behalf of the growth and development of children. In order to do this I will be visiting and observing your classes regularly. I will meet with you individually and as a group to discuss our mutual reactions and concerns about all aspects of the school's operation. You have been here a lot longer than I, so I'll count on you to fill me in on all aspects of the program that you're proud of and want perpetuated. I feel that I, too, have some philosophies and programs which have been successful. Together we'll try to merge the best of all of our experiences with children. We all care very deeply about the quality of instruction we provide to children, and I will do everything I can to protect and enhance the contribution that each of you make to that end. I know how difficult and demanding teaching can be, and there may be some days when it just may not seem to be worth the effort. I will try to be available, to listen, and to provide support to you in tough situations. Now, please tell me how you feel about my comments. Please share your experiences, and tell me where and how I can be helpful."

After a short silence, Peter, the union representative and a third grade teacher in the building for the past seventeen years, said, "This observation process is completely different than our prior experience and I'm not sure that this departure from past practice is acceptable within the context of the collective bargaining contract." John responded, "Any guidance that you can give me to insure that I do not violate the contract will be gratefully received. Perhaps you can fill me in on what concerns you about the observation process. If this is different from your past experiences I suspect all of you (speaking to the other teachers) may have some questions."

Another teacher described experiences at another school in which the principal had operated more as a "snoopervisor" than a supervisor. Most teachers felt that all the principal was doing was checking up on them. After an observation, they usually received a memo outlining what was wrong in their classrooms. A third teacher described a similar experience in which feedback from the principal was experienced as a form of punishment.

I said "Given those experiences I can understand why you may all be concerned about a change in procedures. I'm glad that Peter raised the question so directly. Let me explain how I view the observation process which is somewhat different from your other experiences. I see observation, in part, as helping me to perform my evaluative role which includes identifying your areas of strength as well as areas for further development. I also view it as a way I can become more familiar with your work so that I can be helpful to you in your own continuing development.

I want to be sure that each of you knows that your efforts with children will be acknowledged when they are noteworthy and that we'll work together to improve areas that require refinement or change. I will have expectations regarding your teaching effectiveness, but each of you will know what these expectations are and will participate in the process to set reasonable goals and objectives. You, too, will have expectations for me and I encourage you to demand that I provide the kind of collaborative assistance that you require. Surely, formal observations will be conducted only within the constraints of the contractual agreement.

No doubt each teacher heard and interpreted John's comments differently. Depending on the previous experiences each of them had with principals, some may view this as a positive path to growth. Other teachers may see this as a threat and they may look to Peter to help defend them from John's intrusion. As John develops a group of positive comments on each teacher, resistance will decline. However, if he does not follow through with his commitment, criticism will follow in spite of the sense of relief that may exist. Peter began the process of testing John with the comment on the contract. John will be able to use this first meeting to begin to analyze the obstacles which are likely to impede relationship development and communication. Peter's feelings can be explored during individual sessions to determine whether there are fear factors associated with the externally projected anger.

John began the contracting process with an invitation for comments on his views of supervision. He accepted help from the union representative but would not relent on his commitment to observe teachers. He described the circumstances under which he would call them to task and the way he would do it. The contracting process is thus begun between John and his staff. This process is not completed in a single meeting. The contract for the supervision relationship will be clarified and refined through daily interaction between John and the teaching staff, and during more formalized supervision conference meetings.

It is particularly important to note the support that John committed himself to provide to his teachers. A major contribution that the principal can make is through the ability to empathize with the feelings of teachers. This skill, described more completely in Chapter 3, involves the capacity to feel what the teacher is experiencing as closely as possible and to communicate that feeling in as many ways as are appropriate to the situation. Respectful silence may convey such empathy in certain contexts. The effort is to genuinely feel, and to sincerely convey, empathy to the individual teacher or to the staff as a whole as is situationally appropriate.

Most teachers have experienced a variety of responses to their feelings by people in positions of authority and these experiences may leave them reluctant to reveal their emotions. Vulnerability is considered a sign of weakness by many in our society. Turning to another for support is also considered an indication of dependency by some people. If the principal is truly open and trustworthy with teachers, he/she may be a valuable source of support when needed. If he/she is not trusted or if he is reluctant to provide support, the supervision relationship may be dealing with the symptoms and never the disease. Such circumstances mean that little real support is available to teachers from the principal and no true growth evoking relationship exists within the supervision process. John is inviting his staff to share their individual frustrations and difficulties with him. John's commitment will surely be tested initially with small issues of little significance. In this way the teachers may determine if he will do as he said he would. If he proves to be trustworthy and teachers experience positive effects with him, greater trust and commitment will follow from the teachers. The opposite is also true, and great care must be taken not to violate the trust and confidence given by the staff.

The role of the principal requires a synthesis of the evaluative and accountability function with the supportive function—providing positive regard, taking time to listen attentively, and responding with sincere empathy to the feelings and emotions of teachers. Such an investment will return great dividends when all of the systems in the school feel they have collectively met the goals and objectives which have been set in behalf of school improvement. Through the daily routine of school,

John's contract with the teachers will be tested as the purpose, role, and authority of his supervision relationship are clarified.

It is important to note that the principal must not see himself as having all the answers to staff problems. He must see himself in a collegial supportive role where both teaching and learning are taking place simultaneously. This calls for a process of mutual problem solving where both parties provide input and seek solutions. Some principals may be reluctant to offer such support to teachers fearing that they may not have all the answers. Providing support to teachers means being there to listen and helping them to find solutions together. Consider the alternatives if the principal does not accept this role. Either problems go unsolved or other sources such as the teachers union may be sought out for help. In any case, both the principal and the teachers have much to gain by the development of a clear supervision contract. Within such structure, great freedom can be derived from which mutual growth and satisfaction can be experienced by teacher and principal. The price for avoiding a clear working relationship may include lower levels of performance, greater absenteeism, lower morale, and a less vibrant and enthusiastic teaching staff.

Figure 2.0 indicates some of the frequent obstacles arising in the preparatory and beginning phases of supervision. Contextual considerations and action strategies are also given.

Figure 2.0.
FREQUENT OBSTACLES IN THE
PREPARATORY AND BEGINNING PHASES

Obstacles	Contextual Considerations	Action Strategies
Stalled/Negative Communication	Fear of revealing Ignorance, Incompetence Lack of experience Dynamics of New Relationships	Tuning in, Openess, Honesty, Preparatory Empathy,
Tenuous/Strained Relationships	Authority Issues: — prevalence of indirect communication — fear of confrontation	Trust, Reaching for Concerns, Contracting Clarifying,
Isolation of Teachers	Idiosyncratic Nature of teaching	Peer Commun- ication
Avoidance of Work	Taboo against revealing vulnerability Use of jargon to avoid direct discussion	Reaching for Concerns Demand for Work, Hold the Focus
Systems Conflict	Ambiguity of Role/ Function vis a vis Policy/Board	Define Roles Purposes

Chapter 3

THE NEW PRINCIPAL:
SOME VARIATIONS ON THE THEME

In the previous chapter, examples were presented which illustrated the importance of tuning-in and responding directly to indirect cues. The critical aspects of contracting were also illustrated in the issues of purpose, role, authority, reaching for feedback, and establishing expectation and commitment from teachers. Although the reality of each school situation may have unique aspects, the following examples illustrate the same skills and dynamics in a number of different situations. The underlying problems in these examples represent frequent questions from principals and teachers in workshops. They include a new principal who is promoted from within the staff and has to deal with teachers with whom she had close association. Other examples describe principals who were hired for the expressed purpose of removing the "dead wood."

FROM TEACHER TO PRINCIPAL

The change from classroom teacher to building principal is both exciting and difficult for the incumbent and the staff. The fact that great effort, time, and energy went into the process of acquiring the position does not change the anxiety felt when that fateful first day as principal arrives. Doubts and fears about competency are common in such situations as the new principal recalls the recent past when the behavior of the previous principal was scrutinized in great detail. The usual feelings toward the principal are all too familiar as the new principal can remember having experienced these same feelings. The new principal feels a slight twinge as he/she enters the teachers' room for the first time in the role and there is a sudden silence. Are the teachers talking about me, he/she wonders?

The issues can be more complicated if the new principal was promoted from within the staff. Maureen, a newly appointed elementary principal, reported in an administrative staff meeting that she faced difficult social relationships with two of her former colleagues who were candidates for the job. Maureen was somewhat surprised by her selection, as the other two candidates were both more experienced male teachers. She sensed deep resentment when the news filled the building that she was selected. One of the other candidates assured her that he would help every way possible while the other said nothing. When other principals in the meeting were asked to give her suggestions, one asked if she was sure that she wanted the job. Maureen's greatest fear was having to provide instructional supervision to the remaining losing candidate who had said nothing to her. She worried that he would be uncooperative or downright resistant. In addition, Eloise, the school secretary, had the reputation of being a tyrant who kept everyone in line. It was agreed to look at each problem to develop alternatives.

Social Relationships with Staff Members

Maureen began with staff associations, a particularly painful area. She explained that she had been part of a small group of teachers who had coffee, lunch, and drinks after work on Fridays. Shopping trips and bowling regularly marked the out-of-school group contacts. All this had come to an abrupt halt from the moment she had become principal. Suddenly, she felt no thought was given to her as she ate alone and no invitation to drinks was extended when Friday came. Maureen did not want to try to reenter her social group by asking because she feared rejection. Joking with her former colleagues, she was referred to as "the boss" in a way which she felt demonstrated their preference for the newly developed distance between them. At this point, Maureen was too uncomfortable to pursue the matter and she was fearful of being seen as wanting to push herself on them.

Everyone in the administrative staff meeting agreed that steps had to be taken to deal with the stress and discomfort in the situation. The dilemma of wanting friendships while holding the leadership position with the same teachers was not uncommon. The other administrators in the meeting volunteered to role play how Maureen might approach the problem using the skill of tuning in. The role play follows:

Maureen: I want to talk about something on my mind since becoming principal. Our friendship has changed and I miss the close association which we had for many years. I have worried that I will not be able to still be your friend and do this job. I value your friendship too much to lose it so quickly. Do you feel that we can work out our friendship with me as principal? I sure hope some of you have ideas as to how we can because I miss our association.

Jerine: We noticed a distance between us but we thought that was your preference with your position as principal.

Cassy: It is uncomfortable talking about some things when you are around now. We just can't feel free to speak about lots of things now that you are the principal. We feel like it's squealing to tell you all the dirt.

Maureen: You know I have the same feeling and I recognize that I am responsible for some of the things that you are referring to.

Jerine: Maybe we can figure out how we can be friends and still work with you as principal. We need to decide what is off limits to discuss with you, and try to do the same things we used to do. Let's start by having lunch together.

Cassy: I am glad that you still want to be friends with us.

Maureen realized that she worried so much about the direct discussion that she had avoided it. After the role play she felt comfortable enough to try to approach her old colleagues and work out a way to be friends again. She said that she recognized that the role of principal changed her associations profoundly but that now she realized that she did not have to give up her personal relationships completely.

Avoiding Stereotypes in Working with Staff

Maureen approached her second and third problems using the same skills. Using tuning-in and role playing skills practiced in the administrative staff meeting, Maureen approached the problems. The secretary, Eloise, had the previous principal running around trying to keep peace when relations got rough. Maureen had achieved an uneasy truce with her when she was a teacher. Since becoming the principal, Maureen noticed Eloise had become quite reserved toward her, as though she were "waiting for the other shoe to drop."

Maureen stated that she addressed the problem directly: "I asked Eloise to explain how we could work together now that I was the principal. I told her that I noticed tension in the building between her and the teachers but that one secretary for forty-five staff members was no easy task. She said that everyone wants their work done now while the others wait. Eloise said the teachers pressure her to complete everything yesterday.

I told her I recognized that she was caught in the middle trying to please teachers, answer the phone, and talk to parents. She had a very demanding job for which few people showed any gratitude. I asked Eloise what I could do to improve the situation. She replied that a parent volunteer or two would be a big help. I asked her why a volunteer had not been used in the past. Eloise said that the previous principal felt that too much sensitive information would leak into the rumor mill. I asked if she could select the kind of volunteer that could handle confidential information about children. She said that she knew two retired teachers that would be excellent volunteers." We agreed to arrange a meeting with them as soon as possible.

The important element in this interview is that Maureen did not treat Eloise as if she fit the stereotype that she was rumored to be. If she had treated Eloise as a tyrant with a personality problem, it is highly likely that Eloise would have behaved as if she had such a problem. To avoid such a self-fulfilling prophesy is infinitely better than to fall victim to the vicious cycle that it offers. Thus Maureen was able to reach for a positive response and work toward a better situation. Maureen also prevented Eloise from treating her as a stereotype by working toward a solution. Each treated the other as a person with feelings and needs instead of a one dimensional stereotype.

This example illustrates the value of not accepting the rumored description of anyone. Applying the skills of tuning-in and reaching for feelings, it may be possible to avoid the self-fulfilling prophesy and improve the situation for all concerned. The use of these skills by the principal will not always evoke the desired positive response. It was Edwin A. Locke (1979, 64) who claimed that "a supervisor can help fulfill an employee's desires but he cannot provide him with desires; he can offer him new knowledge or the chance to gain new knowledge but he cannot force him to learn; he can assign goals to a worker but he cannot compel him to accept those goals." It must be recognized that teacher supervision is interactional in nature. Both parties to the process must contribute for it to work well. It is possible to conceive of situations where in spite of skillful behavior by the principal, the teacher does not respond. The focus of the next section is on how the principal can insure that every effort is made to achieve effective results.

Continued Resistance from Staff Members

The problem of continued resistance is illustrated when Maureen attempted to work with Peter, the other candidate for principal who was bitter about not getting the job. Maureen described her efforts to the administrative group. His reactions to her varied from being distant to showing outright hostility. She never considered Peter to be warm but this cool hard disregard left her both hurt and uncomfortable. It was as though he blamed her for him not getting the job. Maureen described her efforts to confront him using the skills of tuning in and reaching for feelings as follows: "I asked Peter to stop by my office after school dismissal so we could talk. He missed the meeting and later said that he had forgotten. I asked if we could meet that day and he said that he was busy and that a day next week would be better. I asked if Tuesday was ok and he agreed. That Tuesday he was fifteen minutes late saying that he had a student who needed extra help. We went to my office and I noticed him looking at the clock. He seemed to avoid eye contact with me and appeared distant. I explained that we needed to work out a way to work together since I was feeling that he was trying to avoid talking to me. He said there was no need for us to discuss the issue as he had no difficulty in accepting me as the building principal. He further said that the former principal respected his competence as a teacher and let him teach as he saw fit. I felt at this point that we were getting nowhere. I leveled with him and told him that I noticed his cool demeanor toward me since I became principal and that I was worried about what it meant. He told me that he had no idea what I was talking about as he was not angry at me though he did feel that he was not given fair treatment by the primarily female selection committee. I asked him how that would affect him. He said that he did not want to talk about it and that if I had any questions about his teaching, he would discuss them. I asked him if we could work together to develop and refine his teaching skills.

He responded that his work was far better than most and if I had any problems with it to so specify. If not, please leave him alone. He further said that he had far more experience than I and that he did not need my suggestions.

He went on to say that if I felt people were angry with me for my getting the job, that was my problem and to leave him out of it. I could see that he was really angry now. I told him my concern was working with him. He said that if I just left him alone, there would be no problems. I told him that he must respect the proprietary interest that my role as principal required me to play and that he would be given the same structure and freedom to make classroom decisions as other teachers in this building. I fully recognized his excellent experience and well-respected teaching skills. I would be observing him within two weeks and I hoped that he would recognize the responsibility we both had to work together. He responded with one word, fine. I thanked him for being frank as he left my office."

Although Maureen felt that she made very little progress with Peter in this session, some important issues were clarified. A very difficult subject had been broached and the deep emotions within it were brought out in the open. Peter had become quite angry while simultaneously denying that he felt anger at all. It was possible that he was never in touch with his true feelings about the situation and that he meant the denial. Peter may subsequently realize his anger and be more free to openly discuss it.

Maureen had confronted the issue of developing a relationship that would permit them to work together, and the fact that he would be treated like every other teacher in the building. The effect here was to insure that he clearly understood that she would not be intimidated and that he could not pressure her into leaving him alone. It was important for Peter to know that she would not be deterred from her responsibility as principal to supervise him and that he was going to have to work with her, one way or the other. At the same time that she clarified their working contract, she offered recognition and showed her respect for his expertise and skill as a teacher. Although his feelings may have made it hard for him to fully accept these compliments from Maureen, he needed to hear them.

Maureen was credited by the group for having the courage to face Peter openly and confront the issues between them. It is important to recognize that the situation with him is far from over. The interactions to come are going to determine whether Maureen can achieve a delicate balance between supportive empathy and demanding expectations for his professional growth. It should be noted that Maureen heard Peter's comment about the "female selection committee" and understood the implied sexist connotation. He was suggesting that she had obtained the job because of her gender. She was not able to respond to this comment at this time, partly because it had strong emotional impact. It may have been just as well to stay focused on the issue of how they would work together for this discussion. However, Maureen would need to be tuned in to this theme and be prepared to challenge it if it emerged again.

Maureen's concluding comment was interesting. She said that she feared the confrontation so much that her anxiety became a real obstacle to both a meeting and to daily communication with Peter. It seemed that the actual confrontation was not nearly as difficult as she feared it would be.

Avoiding the "Removing the Dead Wood" Syndrome

A new principal hired from outside the school district is often viewed as having a mandate to "remove the dead wood," even when no such direction exists. The outside appointee frequently has a higher degree of suspicion and concern from teachers than may exist with an insider. Familiarity may account for part of this phenomenon. Veteran teachers in an established school will wonder how the new outside principal will judge them and whether he/she will recognize the areas of the program that need improvement. The teaching staff of a school which has been formally or informally considered to be operating poorly is very likely to have its defenses heightened.

A common error made by the new principal in such situations is to lay down the law at the outset. This is often the result of a mandate to "clean up the mess," by the superintendent who may have made such a promise to the school board. Such poor preparation and the perceived need to bring about change may have the effect of heightening the principal's anxiety as well. The expectation for teacher resistance and anger in such situations becomes a self-fulfilling prophesy which results in actions by the principal which, in fact, generates resistance and anger. The new principal is building a trap into which he/she will likely fall victim.

Whatever the rationale for the new principal to lay down the law, it is seldom a wise decision, as illustrated in the following example. East Junior High had its share of problems. Vandals left windows broken nearly every weekend. The custodians complained that keeping up with the destruction inside the building was impossible. Frequent fights in the halls and smoking in the lavatories left the building looking more like a war zone than a school. Damage to cars, anonymous threats to individual teachers by phone, and an atmosphere of general discontent were responsible for the high rate of teacher requests for transfer out of the building. Parent complaints and letters to the editor in the local newspaper were frequent indicators of the disdain felt by many people in the community for the situation at East Junior High School.

The retirement of the incumbent principal and a brief search resulted in the appointment of Jack, former assistant principal in a nearby city high school. Jack knew when he took the job that big changes were expected of him and better discipline was first on the list. He described his first meeting with the teaching staff as tense. Many of the teachers sat with their arms folded as if to say "go ahead, change this place." Jack was determined to make this a model junior high school and he decided to set the standards at the outset. His comments and the teachers' reactions from the meeting follow:

"I explained that the rules in this school were too lax and that enforcement of discipline was everyone's job. I pointed out that we had much tougher students at the high school I left and we were able to maintain order and provide excellent teaching as well. I told them that I wanted this school to be the best in the area and that I was sure it would be soon. I told them that careful rule enforcement would straighten out this building in no time at all and that I was counting on them to do their part."

The response to Jack by the staff was an expressionless silence. He quickly went on to explain the duty roster for the week to come but he sensed the feeling of anger that the teachers radiated. Jack commented that the teachers would hardly talk to him and the whole effort to improve the school seemed to be on his shoulders. He explained that what he wanted was good for the staff but they seemed to not care one way or the other. His work was an uphill struggle all the way.

This is a classic example of a new principal attacking the teachers when they feel most vulnerable. Jack made no effort to recognize the staff contributions and worth. This left them with a choice of rejecting themselves if they supported him. If Jack had worked within the norms of the teachers and slowly worked for mutual recognition of the problems that they faced, he would have had a chance to win their support and accomplish his goals. Hollander (1961) refers to this process as building "idiosyncratic credits." For the teachers to support the new directions, they would have to be part of the process of deciding that indeed a particular problem exists and that the appropriate solution is necessary. This group of teachers needed a great deal of support from the new principal to show that he understood how difficult it had been for them during the past few years. Without this support base for a relationship, he could expect them to behave defensively, as if he were attacking them. Jack may have achieved a different result if he had used another approach. One alternative example follows:

"I know that school has not been easy for any of you during the recent past with the press, parents, and the administration throwing stones from all directions. It is difficult to teach when you're constantly fighting for control with your students. I want to assure you that I need to understand your thoughts about what is and is not going on here and what should be done about it. I want to listen to each of you to learn and understand all perspectives on the operation of this school. Don't worry about me making changes without your support. I realize that only by working together can this school improve. Now it's your turn to speak and I'll listen."

This approach by the principal must be genuine. He indeed must believe that the support of the teachers is absolutely essential to initiate meaningful change. If he supports such beliefs verbally but his actions are unilateral, it is likely that the teachers will react negatively. Fullan (1982), Joyce (1983), Hoy (1986), and many others suggest that it is impossible to make significant changes in schools without the cooperation and support of the teaching staff. The staff at East Junior High has had difficulty setting limits on student behavior. It is imperative that Jack understand as fully as possible why this happened. This is clearly his first step. A principal who simply makes changes with no thought to the effect on the staff is very likely to find a lack of support from teachers when implementation begins. In addition, a principal who was very demanding without providing support to his/her teachers would probably be viewed as harsh and unsympathetic. Jack began with a difficult meeting and now he will attempt to start over with the staff. His second effort follows: "I need to discuss with you the way I began at this school. I should have recognized the pressure I felt to bring about changes and shared that with you, especially since you have been under a similar kind of pressure. Instead, I let my anxiety do the talking with authoritative statements that were completely out of line. I hope you will excuse me for that outburst and let this meeting be the beginning of our relationship. Can we forget that meeting and try to start again?"

This second effort is well worth the investment since the first left Jack in a rather hopeless position. In addition, it is an excellent opportunity for the principal to admit his own mistake. Teachers need to believe that mistakes are part of the process of growth. It is common in our society to mask mistakes, attempting to cover or hide them, instead of using them as opportunities for redirection. This kind of honesty may well enhance the view that teachers have of the principal and help them to see him more clearly as a person.

Perhaps the most difficult problem a new principal may encounter in contracting with the teachers is what has been called a false consensus (Schwartz, 1968). In this situation the principal can raise neither an affirmation or denial of a position by the teachers. The logic of the official position may be so well established that the "rightness" of it prevents any mention of the lurking negative feelings of the staff. In such situations staff members will express their feelings about the issue informally or underground where similar feelings may be found. This means that the principal has lost the ability to communicate openly on this matter with the staff. In such situations, agreement to proceed may be what Schwartz refers to as the "illusion of work," where no real effort to comply with a given direction is taken but everyone verbally assures their compliance. The task of the principal is to reach past such an artificial agreement and to insist that the conversation be real. The hidden, ambivalent, and negative staff feelings must be brought out in the open and discussed. If this does not occur, the emotional underlife of the school may become a force that will resist change and growth. Such circumstances must be avoided by direct confrontation of the issues using the skills suggested: a demand for honesty by the principal.

The preliminary and beginning phases of teacher supervision can help a new principal enter a school and initiate the development of a constructive working relationship. Tuning in is a skill which calls for the development of preparatory empathy. The contracting skills help the principal to clarify the purpose in supervision, to reach for feedback from teachers, and to deal with issues arising from authority. New principals face particular problems whether they have moved from the classroom to the position within the same school, or they have been hired from outside the district. The following chapters examine the middle, or work, phase of teacher supervision. A model of the work phase is introduced with a number of common problems to illustrate the skills in practice.

Chapter 4

SESSIONAL TUNING–IN AND CONTRACTING SKILLS WITH TEACHERS IN THE WORK PHASE

The work phase of teacher supervision follows contracting or clarification of the working contract in the beginning phase. It consists of the steps in completing the contract for supervision developed in the beginning phase and is often more complicated than the first two phases. The work phase of teacher supervision is the most enduring because it exists within the daily routine of school operations throughout the year. The focus of the work phase of teacher supervision is the process of instruction which may be taken for granted easily as the routine aspects of school are handled superficially. The commonplace activities of dealing with the operation of the school may completely occupy the principal's attention and the issue of the improvement of teaching skills and/ or professional growth for teachers, may be overlooked and/or left unattended.

In addition, as other priorities such as budgeting, committee assignments, and other matters come to the principal's attention, the temptation to ignore subtle clues of teacher supervision problems is increased. A problem such as a teacher who is constantly screaming at children to maintain control in the classroom, may not be serious enough to attract the attention of the principal. Occasional complaints about teachers by students and parents may have the same effect. The principal may relegate such matters to the category of "leave it alone and maybe it will go away." Such a policy is particularly tempting to the principal with many activities taking place in the building for which he/she has ultimate responsibility.

One dilemma that may compound the "let it be" philosophy is the accumulation of small, unattended problems or issues which may become troublesome when that teacher's formal evaluation is undertaken. It can be difficult because the principal's concern may be viewed as inappropri-

40

ate if such information is discussed since it raises the question, "why was it overlooked until now?" Further, if the information is overlooked entirely, the principal may be viewed as misfeasant, especially if more significant issues concerning poor performance are raised with that teacher at a later date. The superintendent may suggest that prompt attention to the problem at an earlier time may have prevented it from becoming severe.

It may be taken as a given that teachers seldom ask to be supervised and expressions of such need are likely to be indirect if they are made at all. This fact, combined with the illusion of work, described in the previous chapter, may cause the principal to ignore the supervision needs of teachers while maintaining the outward appearance of business as usual. With these issues in mind, this chapter examines the particular dynamics of the work phase of teacher supervision. A model is presented describing the communication, relationship, and problem-solving skills used in the work phase of teacher supervision to guide the explanation and examples. Common school situations are used to illustrate the model and the skills. The dynamics of the problems between teachers and the principal serve to illustrate the application or the nonapplication of the skills of the work phase of supervision.

The Work Phase of Teacher Supervision

The skills of the work phase, adapted from the helping professions and the work of Shulman (1982) and Schwartz (1976), and grouped in categories referred to as skills, are intended for application to daily problems of school operation and specifically to teacher supervision. The skills are composed of closely related subskills or behaviors in which the principal's intent is the common element. The model of the work phase of teacher supervision in Figure 4.1 contains empathic skills which are all behaviors related to the principal's efforts to deal with the affective and emotional aspects of teachers' responses.

The work phase skills in teacher supervision and the model in Figure 4.0 are intended for application to single conferences, or meetings. Each individual conference or meeting, regardless of the number of teachers involved with the principal, is viewed as a session. Thus the skills suggested are as applicable to a post-observation conference with one teacher as they are to a staff meeting with the entire building faculty. Since these are viewed as single sessions, the term sessional is used with the related skills in the model. Adaptations of the tuning in and contracting skills of the beginning phase are used in the work phase of teacher supervision. Sessional ending skills are described at the end of this chapter.

In similar fashion with the preliminary phase, prior to a conference with an individual teacher, or a meeting with a group of teachers in the work phase, the principal tunes in to potential concerns which may arise in the session. The preliminary effort here involves the principal using sessional tuning in to develop empathy for the feelings of teachers and in preparation for indirect expressions of such feelings. As in the beginning phase, the principal attempts to examine his/her own feelings as well. The effort to develop empathy also provides the principal with the opportunity to consider a variety of direct responses which may be appropriate when respective indirect cues arise in the session. Such preparation helps to insure that the principal is ready with appropriate responses to issues which may have become obstacles to effective supervision work with teachers.

Figure 4.0
A MODEL OF THE WORK PHASE

Sessional Tuning-in Skills
Sessional Contracting Skills
Elaborating Skills
Empathic Skills
Skills in Sharing Feelings
Skills in Making a Demand for Work
Skills in Defining Obstacles
Skills in Sharing Data
Sessional Ending Skills

Sessional Skills

In the beginning of each session, the principal's initial task is to elicit teacher concerns and to use sessional contracting skills to clarify the work at hand. The beginning of the work phase is often a particularly sensitive point where moving too quickly into a planned agenda, or suggesting one, may discourage a teacher or a group of teachers from opening an important issue or pressing concern. An additional danger of agreeing to a solution before it is well understood or fully discussed may occur when the principal moves too quickly in a session with teachers. A major effort must be made by the principal to encourage teachers to explain their true feelings and concerns. The empathic and elaboration skills of the work phase of teacher supervision are useful to the principal to encourage such expression. The principal must also be prepared to share his/her own feelings at the appropriate opportunity to insure that the teachers understand them as well.

The work of teacher supervision is aimed at the evocation of growth, new understanding, or development. Resistance is an inevitable and expected part of the teacher supervision process. Resistance should be regarded by the principal as a healthy sign of teachers trying to reach out for growth while simultaneously feeling the need for security by holding on to what is felt to be comfortable. Such ambivalence is often signaled by teachers' evasive, defensive, or aggressive reactions which may be congruous or incongruous with the circumstances of the session. It is at this juncture that the principal, understanding the significance of the resistance, may need to make a demand for work in order to help the teacher or teachers take the important next steps.

The principal must be aware of obstacles which may deter the growth process throughout the work phase of teacher supervision. Teachers reactions to the demands of the principal, for example, may generate antipathy which, if left unattended, can negatively affect the supervisory relationship. Such obstacles must be understood by the principal and discussed openly in order to keep teachers from operating under the surface where these obstacles may become more powerful as unspoken points of mutual agreement. Such points may not be noticed or appropriately dealt with by the unknowing principal. Open discussion of the feelings and concerns of teachers is the means by which the principal points out and deals with obstacles to growth in the work phase of supervision.

Teachers must have complete access to the principal's data base on the issues involved in the work in order for them to fully understand, support the need for, and be willing to take appropriate action on those issues. It is absolutely critical that the principal understand that how this information is shared is as important as the implications of its meaning. The data sharing skills of the principal enable teachers rather than weaken them. Avoiding the pitfalls of self-rejection affords teachers a means of accepting suggestions without bitterness.

Sessional ending skills are the means by which the principal insures that gains made in the work phase of teacher supervision are not lost. Agreements made in the work phase must be monitored and adjustments are often necessary. The specific steps for implementation that follow the session are the object of the ending skills.

This model of the work phase of supervision is relevant to all forms of interaction which the principal may have with teachers. The skills which have been suggested for a postobservation conference can be applied to a brief encounter with a teacher anywhere in the school building. It must also be noted that the skills seldom proceed as directly as just described. The principal will use skills as the situation suggests rather than in a particular sequence. For example, in the effort to clarify the work, both empathic and elaboration skills may be used.

Sessional Tuning-In Skills

Sessional tuning in follows the same purposes as the beginning phase except that the principal localizes his focus to the individual teacher or group, the immediate circumstances, and the purposes of the session. These parameters assist the principal in narrowing the focus to more precisely fix the issues, feelings, and concerns of the teachers involved and the potential effects that they may have on the work to be accomplished. This effort by the principal is applicable to every encounter he/she may have with teachers no matter how brief. Empathy is an essential and fundamental element in the supervisory relationship between the principal and the teachers. It serves as part of the baseline from which trust and respect may be generated.

While tuning in is an important skill for all encounters, the reality of the stress of the principal's job must be taken into account. The principal is responsible for administrative matters, the coordination of activities of many staff members, as well as maintaining relationships with parents' groups, the school board, etc. It is unrealistic to expect the principal to be able to tune in to teachers at all times. Often, it is at the end of the day or in later reflection that the principal is able to consider an earlier incident and return to a teacher to reopen discussion. Teachers also have a professional responsibility to be more direct in their communications. Once a principal has created a climate in the school which conveys an openness to difficult communications to teachers, it is not unreasonable to expect them to take some responsibility for their part in the interaction.

There are particular times, however, when a principal needs to take the risk of it going badly.

As an example, consider the difficulty a principal faces when an unpopular policy is implemented by the central office. Budget cuts are an example where the principal must explain the teacher position reductions which follow a failed referendum. In such a situation the principal, feeling caught between the central office and the teachers, may arrange the agenda of a faculty meeting so as to leave little time to discuss adverse reactions by teachers. This is usually a fundamental error as the reactions of teachers are likely to emerge later in various forms. Militant attitudes, excessive use of sick and/or personal leave days, or a reduced commitment to the school programs are potential manifestations of such feeling.

A fundamental postulate of the interactional practice theory presented here is that teachers' feelings are a major contributor to their behavior. These feelings must be considered and discussed openly by the principal no matter how sensitive they may be. Such honest and real communication with the principal may be the only way teachers can get past adverse feelings and reactions to freely approach the work at hand. Underlying antipathy is an obstacle which, if left unattended, may increase and subsequently block growth and development for teachers and the school.

A principal may be tuned in to an issue and the underlying feelings but not feel comfortable about opening "Pandora's Box." The concern may be that teachers will accept an invitation to discuss feelings of anger, depression, being burned out, etc., and that the discussion will lead to greater immobilization of both staff and the principal. It is important to recognize that feelings are always dealt with in the pursuit of purpose. There is specific work to be done at faculty meetings designed to help teachers to do their job. Ventilation of emotion or affect by itself is not sufficient. Staff need to be helped to examine what can be done to buffer stress from a problem or what steps might be taken to influence a decision or a policy. A crucial issue in situations such as these is the principle of the "next step." No matter how bad a situation may be, there is always a next step.

For example, the principal, in dealing with the problem of teacher position reductions due to budget cuts, needs to focus on the particular effects that such reductions are likely to have on his/her staff. Tuning in to teachers' anger about this situation and to their underlying feelings which are not often openly expressed is an effective way to encourage such expression. Teachers in such circumstances may feel that the community does not value their dedication or service to children. In addition, budget cuts may mean an increase in class sizes, or a change in the way teachers work by reducing or eliminating planning time.

The results may leave teachers feeling less valued and the principal needs to assure them that this is not necessarily the case. Involving parents in such efforts may help teachers recognize the mindless nature of school budget defeats while assuring them that their work with children is truly valued and appreciated. The principal must also help the teachers to discuss the reality of the situation and the measures that they need to take to minimize the impact on the operation of the school. Such communication is vital to a healthy and positive school climate in which teachers are motivated to continue the effort to develop the instructional program and to refine their teaching skills.

The principal must carefully consider the effects that such changes have on the faculty. When abrupt change is unavoidable and teachers are required to master unfamiliar practices such as much larger classes or a much wider range of ability in their students, their perceived need to maintain a professional image may mask their fears. They may voice vehement feelings about other real, but less significant, issues as an expression of such underlying anxiety.

Teachers in one school, for example, explained that moving to heterogeneous grouping would force them to find busy work for the brighter students while basic instruction was being carried out with slower students. The effect was to slow the pace of the brighter students thus permitting the slower students to keep up. Although there is an element of truth in their feelings, the underlying problem was that homogeneous grouping had been used for so long that teachers were comfortable with the teaching procedures and the results achieved. They were concerned that the new grouping procedures would require new teaching approaches and ultimately produce diminished results by comparison.

When the principal reached past the initial objections, he found teachers fearful that bright students may not achieve as well as they had in the past, and that their teaching techniques needed refinement. Once this issue was on the table, the principal was able to ask teachers to tap their fund of experience for ideas about how they might cope with the changed situation. Supervisors often feel that they must be the source of answers in a difficult situation and fail to utilize the resources within their own staff.

In addition, in this case, the principal provided some of his own ideas and connected his staff to resources from other schools. He suggested that curriculum materials, texts, and inservice programs could be surveyed to secure the most appropriate match with the new grouping procedures. Tuning in to these concerns before the meeting, he invited a teacher in to speak who was from a neighboring district where this change had been made two years earlier. After the meeting, teachers were more inclined to view the change positively. These issues may never have been fully discussed in a faculty meeting if the principal had not tuned in to the likely concerns of the teachers in this situation. The principal's ability to tune in to staff feelings, particularly in adverse situations, serves as an effective link to teacher motivation and behavior. Antipathy in such situations may be prevented from becoming an obstacle to teacher effectiveness. In all cases, the skill of tuning in begins with the principal examining his/her own feelings on the issue at hand which often are congruent with those of the teachers involved.

The parallel process is evident in this example as well. When teachers are concerned about the impact of changes in class size due to budget cuts, there may be similar concerns on the part of students. Both those students who need more attention just to keep pace and those who feel held back may send indirect cues of their concerns to teachers. These cues may emerge in the form of apathy, boredom, absenteeism, or acting-out behavior. Unless the principal is tuned in to the feelings of the teachers, there is some likelihood that the teachers will miss the signals from the students. Part of the technical discussion of how to handle an adaptation to larger class sizes might focus on how to deal with the indirectly expressed concerns of the students.

The principal may not be able to be continuously tuned in to the meaning of every indirect cue. Teachers in such situations may give many opportunities by repeating the cues until a response is obtained, or they may give up trying. The principal may be well advised to respond to the cues, since dealing with the results of neglecting the problem may be more time consuming and difficult than anticipating it. Principals must decide whether they truly want to deal with teachers' adverse feelings. This is the first step toward extending the principal's capacity for using tuning-in skills.

A principal's willingness to hear the negatives from her/his faculty will often be directly related to whether or not she/he feels there is an administrator willing to hear the principal's stress. It is difficult to feel "caught in the middle" with no place to go.

Sessional Contracting Skills

In similar fashion with tuning-in, sessional contracting attempts to focus on the particular agenda items which are relevant to the immediate individual conference or group meeting with teachers. Using the contracting skills, the principal introduces the items he/she proposes for discussion while asking teachers to suggest items of concern to them. This open agenda formation allows teachers to place urgent concerns and questions on the table for discussion. This procedure is a substantial indication to teachers that their feelings are important and that faculty meetings belong to them as well as to the principal. Teacher ambivalence may be somewhat neutralized by the collective attention directed toward their concern when the principal uses this technique to formulate the agenda for the session.

When teachers are given the opportunity to vent feelings and concerns which trouble them at the beginning of a session, they may be more likely to freely invest themselves in the other items on the agenda. For example, teachers may read in the morning paper that state reimbursements to school districts were reduced by the legislature. The teachers' room buzzes all day with talk of the reductions in force that may be forthcoming. The issue can hardly be avoided that afternoon at the faculty meeting and business cannot proceed as usual. In particular, the junior members of the faculty have grave concerns about their continued employment. Family disruption and other important concerns may act as obstacles which prevent or reduce a teacher's capacity to respond to topics on the agenda. Discussion may take place but no real commitment to the matters at hand exists because the real agenda lies under the surface and all of the teachers' energy is committed there. The principal may not recognize the circumstances for what they are—the illusion of work where no real communication takes place.

Instead of proceeding as if the issue did not exist, recognizing the pressing concerns of teachers may be enough to free them to consider other items on the agenda. When it is not possible to provide direct information to meet the concerns of teachers, it is wise to agree to define their problems and obtain the most accurate information possible by a reasonable date. This may allow them to hold their anxiety in abeyance until accurate information is available. Assuring them that they will be given the best information as soon as possible may be the only course of action available to the principal. This alternative may ultimately prove to be more fruitful than avoiding the issue in preference to covering the published agenda.

Sessional contracting with the group is an effort by the principal to include teachers' concerns on the agenda for discussion. The desired effect is to foster real conversation with teachers representing authentic commitment to the work at hand. The principal must be alert to indirect cues representing teacher concerns and he/she must be ready to provide direct responses to such indirect cues, thus insuring that the real agenda is not left under the surface of the discussion. The principal must resist the temptation to offer immediate answers until he/she knows exactly what concerns them. Initially, a tentative posture may be most useful to the principal attempting to clarify the working contract for the immediate session at hand. The principal attempting to elicit teacher concerns may use elaboration skills to obtain the real message from teachers.

Figure 4.1 lists some of the frequent obstacles in the work phase. Contextual considerations and action strategies are also given.

Figure 4.1
FREQUENT OBSTACLES IN THE WORK PHASE

OBSTACLES	CONTEXTUAL CONSIDERATIONS	ACTION STRATEGIES
Temptation to defer responsibilities	Multifaceted responsibilities	Work phase model
Stalled progress Negative reactions to demand for work	Ambivalence about change/growth	Demand for work "process" the obstacle
Indirect expression of concerns	Dynamics of silences Illusion of work	Reach inside silences
Lack of participation	Inadequate preparation of supervisor	Development of communication relationship skills: Tuning-in; reach for feedback; Clarify work at hand
Underlying antipathy	Unattended issues create anger/resistance Feelings as contributors to behavior	Refocus tasks Explore barriers; Open discussion; Principal's data base must be shared with staff
Ambivalence about programs	Need for inclusion Tendency to engage in fruitless speculation	Mutual agenda-setting; Reach for concerns; Problem definition; Alert to indirect cues; Resist giving quick answers

Chapter 5

ACKNOWLEDGING FEELINGS WITH TEACHERS

Elaborating Skills

The principal uses elaborating skills to help teachers explain their concerns. Difficulty in communication may stem from many sources including anxiety from the role differences between teacher and principal and a lack of clear understanding of the concern by the teacher. A variety of elaboration skills are available to the principal to clarify teacher concerns including moving from the general to the specific, containment, focused listening, questioning, and reaching inside silences.

Moving from the General to the Specific

When teachers explain a general concern that is related to a specific situation, the principal should view their comments as opening statements. Often teachers see the event in general terms because they may have experienced it that way. Generality may also convey fundamental ambivalence which a teacher may feel about the situation. Consider the example in which a teacher brings a problem concerning a parent to the principal. Note the global terms used by the teacher to express the problem with a defensive parent:

Angela, a new fourth-grade teacher in the building, began the conference by saying that some parents just refuse to support efforts to help their children with school projects. She went on to say that she would like to discuss a problem she was having with Mrs. Marshall, a very defensive parent. When I asked her to explain what she meant, she said that she needed help getting a parent to admit that she was not providing the support that her son needed to complete a library project which was also assigned to every other student in the class. I explained that such defensive behavior usually means that the parent was threatened and she is behaving normally.

Angela looked doubtful, and I asked her if she agreed with me. She said that some parents would not accept responsibility for helping with school work and they should be made aware of the difficulty faced by the child in such circumstances.

At this point in our discussion, Angela is no better off for having talked about her problem. Note the broad generality in the comments and the lack of direction or alternatives for action with Mrs. Marshall. The following conclusion to the conference illustrates increasi g specificity.

Principal: Angela, it sounds as if you have a difficult situation with Mrs. Marshall. Tell me exactly what was said by each of you in your meeting.

Teacher: Mrs. Marshall seemed distant and defensive from the beginning of the conference. I explained that parents in our class were expected to help with school projects and that her son needed her support to successfully complete his work on the library project. Mrs. Marshall responded smugly that she was not able to provide the help to her son because she was too busy.

Principal: Were you feeling angry with her because of her attitude and lack of willingness to help her son?

Teacher: Exactly! I was thinking that if she feels this way about the project, it's no wonder that her son's homework and much of his school-work is poorly done. She simply doesn't care about her son's education. Such people should not have children.

Principal: It sure is easy to understand why you feel anger with Mrs. Marshall for neglecting her son. I wonder if you were supporting her son during the conference, who was helping her? She is a widowed parent with four children and she has two jobs to make ends meet.

Teacher: Mrs. Marshall never told me about her home.

Principal: Maybe she feels guilty about not helping her son, but she may not see you as helping her. Perhaps your approach and the circumstances made her feel that you were judging her harshly so she became defensive. She will need your support and understanding to let the barriers down. If you want her to be more understanding about her son's needs for help with school work, you may need to be more understanding with her situation.

Teacher: I could talk to her about arranging for her son to work with two other students in order to reduce the trips to the library. I could also ask her if she would like me to check with other parents and make an effort to arrange a car pool with her. I sure wish I knew her situation before we met.

The principal persisted in getting the details of the meeting between he parent and the teacher. The general discussion turned into an examination of the specific comments and details involved in the situation. Moving from the general to the specific helped the principal to help the teacher analyze the interaction with the parent more carefully. Often the emotions in such situations have a powerful generalizing effect which may reduce the ability of the people involved to understand those effects, particularly those involving the other person. The principal may move from the general to the specific and back to the general again to facilitate the teachers' understanding of the situation. A crucial element of this encounter was the principal's willingness to understand the feelings of the teacher. Without this empathy, the principal would be in the position of asking the teacher to understand the stresses of the parent while simultaneously modeling the opposite behavior in relation to the teacher.

Containment: Not Giving Answers

When teachers explain a problem to the principal, there may be a great temptation to give an answer, even in the middle of the question. The need to do so may be related to the principal's desire to be helpful, supportive, and knowledgeable with his/her staff. This may be particularly true of a new principal trying to make the right impression. The problem arises when the suggestion is directed at the question but not at the real concern of the teacher. A cautious effort to listen completely to the teacher helps to determine whether the question is really deeper than it may have appeared.

The following occurred in a school in which teachers agreed to analyze their own teaching using a video-recording camera mounted on a mobile cart. Teachers were to sign a roster indicating which day they would use the camera to record a teaching segment. This procedure was part of the self-analysis they agreed to complete. The principal noticed that Mrs. Rugins had not signed up to use the VCR and he attempted to overcome her resistance by providing a solution to the problem:

"I explained to Mrs. Rugins that I was concerned that she had not signed up for the VCR. I told her that she was the only teacher in the building who had not used the procedure. She said that it was hard for her to find the time to set up and prepare for the actual segment that she would record. I told her that I would have the cafeteria aide cover for her during the ten or twenty minutes that it would take to prepare for the recording. She agreed that would help and she promised to do her self-analysis soon."

This is an example of the illusion of work in which the teacher provides an artificial agreement designed to get the principal off her back. Neither the principal nor the teacher expected that the task would be completed soon or indeed at all. After a considerable time with no progress, the principal reopened the issue. On this occasion the principal tuned-in to the anxiety felt by Mrs. Rugins. In addition, instead of offering another solution, he contained himself and reached for the deeper concerns behind her resistance:

"When I indicated to Mrs. Rugins that she had still not signed up for the VCR, she apologized and said that she was not good with machines of any kind. She just didn't remember which button to press to record or how to adjust the sound. Resisting the temptation to demonstrate the correct operating procedure for the VCR, I probed deeper into her reluctance by asking if there was something bothering her about this whole videotape business.

There was a long pause, and then she told me she had never been videotaped before and that all the other teachers showed their tapes to their families and each other and she just couldn't face that whole issue. She said she was sure that she would "freeze-up" and do a terrible lesson; then, when the other teachers saw it, she would be humiliated. I told her that I could understand how hard it was to risk her work with colleagues. I tried to reassure her that everyone on the staff had similar teaching difficulties in one area or another. I explained, that I could appreciate her hesitation and that maybe I had to do some work with our whole faculty group on finding a way for us to risk with each other without feeling embarrassment.

In the meantime, I proposed that she take the VCR and I would put it on the slowest recording speed. This would permit her to leave it running for four hours. I suggested that she record an ordinary morning of teaching and then erase all but twenty minutes or so that she could analyze. In this way, she would have ample time to become accustomed to the camera and she would still have the option of using the afternoon if nothing in the morning session pleased her. She said that the ability to leave the camera on for a long period was a big help and that she was sure that she could do it now."

Focused Listening

Often when emotions run high, it can be difficult to zero in on the precise message behind the rhetoric. Even in less emotional discussions the principal often needs to be sure of what a teacher is saying behind the words. Focused listening helps to concentrate on specific parts of a teacher's communication until the principal has the real message. This may mean overlooking the "static" and tuning-in to the main point of the conversation. This is often the case when a visit from the union representative reminds the principal that some aspect of the union contract is not being observed. The smoke may not be where the fire exists. Teachers may not want to openly tell the principal that faculty meetings are too frequently over the time agreed to in the contract. A visit from the union representative may help him to understand this without a confrontation with the building teachers.

Questioning

Questioning is a means of probing into the meaning of the message. The supervisor may obtain additional information which may help to define the nature of the problem through use of questions. When an issue is raised by a teacher, which puts the principal "on the spot," a question may be better than a defensive or aggressive comment made in haste. The principal may respond with "you seem really angry about this, what has upset you?" Questioning offers the teacher a chance to more fully explain the problem. It provides the principal with a better understanding of the problem while affording the opportunity to demonstrate sincere interest by his/her demonstrated attention to the answer. Following his/her question, the principal uses eye contact, facial expressions, and body language to appropriately convey sincere attention to the teacher's response. Albeit these behaviors are important throughout the session, they are absolutely critical in receiving answers to questions.

Reaching Inside Silences

When the principal meets silence in the course of a meeting with a teacher or group, it must be understood accurately. Silence is always carrying a message. The problem is to find the meaning of the message behind the silence. There may be a great temptation to react defensively to silence. Such responses may evoke continuous but progressively less meaningful comments by the principal. Silence may be a trigger which teachers use to get the nervous principal to do all the talking and thus avoid real commitments from them. Continuous use of silence may be a sign of passive anger. Silence must be interpreted with sensitive intuition. This requires the principal to use his/her own feelings as a guide to help unlock its meaning. Unfortunately, most supervisors interpret silence as meaning that they did something wrong. This is ironic, since silence may well mean the supervisor has done something right.

The elaboration skill of reaching inside silences involves probing for its meaning. Silence may be an indication of the effort a teacher is making to consider or think about what has been said. Abrupt silence in a stream of regular conversation may mean the teacher disagrees with the previous comment of the principal or that it was simply not understood. The principal must be flexible in making an effort to define the silence on the chance that his/her interpretation is incorrect. In such situations the principal should encourage the teacher to validate his/her response.

Reaching inside silences may call for a direct question such as "you seem quiet now, is there something we talked about that worries you?" When a traumatic event is explained by a teacher to the principal, silence may convey respect for the depth and the legitimacy of the feelings involved. A comment reflecting the feeling such as, "you have every right to be upset by that," may be appropriate. When silence is used to convey anger the principal may receive abbreviated answers to open-ended questions. The teacher may avoid eye contact or keep checking the time. In such situations it may be a serious mistake to allow the conference to proceed without dealing with the issue.

In such situations the principal may have to probe repeatedly with progressively more specific questions to define the source of the anger. If a fundamental disagreement arises, such as a teacher who feels that the principal has inadequate expertise to properly evaluate his performance, a modification in the working contract is suggested as follows: "Bill, I understand your feeling that I am not a physics teacher and thus lack expertise in your field. However, since we both have a legal obligation to be here, can we agree to try to make the best of the situation and work toward mutual understanding?"

Silences are important sources of meaning in supervision work with teachers. The principal must use his/her own feelings as a guide to explore silences and he/she must be open to the possibility that his/her interpretation is incorrect. Responses to silence must be flexible in order to obtain clarifying information from the teacher in the most appropriate manner possible.

Empathic Skills

An underlying assumption of this model is that the emotions of teachers have a profound effect on their ability to work with children. Unless teachers are able to tune in to their own feelings, and develop the skills for managing their affect and using it professionally, they will not be able to help their students manage their feelings. In turn, managing one's feelings is a crucial step for students increasing their ability to manage their problems (e.g., learning, classroom behavior). The reciprocal interaction between managing feelings and managing problems is at the core of this supervision model. This conclusion supports the incorporation of empathic skills for application by the principal in teacher supervision.

Clearly, if teachers are to be expected to interact positively with children and empathy is part of the foundation for the teacher/student relationship, the principal must model similar practices in his/her work with teachers. The principal cannot tell teachers to treat children humanely, and then behave inappropriately in her/his treatment of teachers. The cornerstone of supportive supervision is the ability of the principal to empathize with teachers. The greater the extent to which the principal provides support to teachers, the more he/she may expect them to provide it to children.

Research support for the value of empathy in work with people is ubiquitous (Flanders, 1970), (Rogers, 1961), (Carkhuff, 1971, 1972), (Shulman, 1991). Fundamental to an effective supervisory relationship with teachers is the provision of support to help them deal with job related stresses. Difficult students, nonsupportive parents, inadequate materials, and large class sizes are a few of the literally countless pressures that may produce stress for teachers. The principal is one of the primary resources to which teachers should be able to turn when these stresses become difficult. He/she responds to such circumstances with empathic skills, demonstrating the capacity to understand teachers' feelings and the ability to communicate that understanding to teachers effectively.

Obstacles to Empathic Responses

The pressures of teaching that lead to stress for teachers are paralleled by similar conditions for the principal. Complaints from parents on everything from too much to too little homework, busses that arrive late or early, accidents and fights on the playground, pressures from the central office for paperwork, budget deadlines, committee assignments, occasional grievances, and many other demands on the principal may be sources of stress. If the principal has no resources to empathize with such stresses, he/she may find progressively less capacity to provide empathy to teachers.

A major source of difficulty in providing empathy to teachers may be the principal's perception of authority. The myth that the principal must avoid familiarity with teachers in order to remain objective is regarded by some to be true. This perception requires the principal to maintain a degree of distance between himself and the teaching staff. Such distance makes the provision of empathy extremely difficult, if not impossible. The required demeanor for this role perception is cold, detached, and clinical. This posture suggests making demands on teachers with no effort to understand their feelings. This situation is a regrettable model to offer teachers when expectations for their work with children are quite the opposite.

Effective teacher supervision requires a judicious blend of both supportive and demanding behaviors from the principal. This suggests a clear mutual understanding of purpose and role, a well constructed relationship based on trust and honesty, and consistent demonstration of the ability to understand and convey empathy to teachers. The mixture of both supportive and demanding aspects of the role of the principal may be the most difficult part of the job.

The use of mundane expressions in efforts to convey empathy, particularly when the empathy is not genuine, may result in shallow responses from teachers, anger, or no response at all. Such terms as "I understand, I see, or I hear what you are saying," when used mechanically, without the principal actually feeling the emotion, is ineffective. Continually paraphrasing teacher concerns, "so you feel that. . . . ," may also be an ineffective means of showing empathy. These techniques may result in anger instead of rapport if care is not taken to assure sincerity. They all tend to convey insincerity whether it is intended or not. Empathy must be genuine to be effective. Three important subskills are incorporated in empathic skills. These subskills are reaching for teachers' feelings, acknowledging teachers' feelings, and putting teachers' feelings into words.

Reaching for Teacher's Feelings

The effort by the principal to reach for teachers' feelings asks them to share the emotional aspects of a message with someone who is sincerely interested. This expression of interest in a teacher must be genuine. The example that follows involves a principal and a teacher whose performance was being affected by illness. After several years of satisfactory service, Joe, the teacher, began to show signs of strange behavior. Complaints by students and parents about needless repetition of previously taught material were frequent. Teachers in rooms connected to Joe's room complained of disruptive behavior and a high noise level. These complaints were very recent and, previously, the principal never had occasion to be concerned about Joe's teaching. During the last week the principal noticed Joe having lunch in his car.

In the middle the second period of this particular schoolday a guidance counselor ran into the principal's office saying several students from Joe's class reported that he had fallen asleep at his desk while the class was doing seatwork. The principal went to investigate immediately. As he entered the room he noticed a strong odor of alcohol and indeed Joe was asleep at his desk. The principal's conference with Joe follows:

Principal: I want to talk with you about your teaching and the difficulties that have surfaced lately with your classes.

Teacher: I know some of my students have complained about my classes lately, but I'm making an effort to concentrate on improving my teaching.

Principal: I am concerned about you. You have been a hard worker on this faculty for a long time and lately you seem distant and troubled. Can you tell me what is wrong?

Teacher: (tears began to fill his eyes) These have been the worst months of my life. My wife left me.

Principal: It must be very difficult for you to cope with your home situation and maintain your teaching duties to your students. Has it been hard for you?

As the remaining empathic skills are explained, this example will be continued. It is important to note that the principal has asked Joe to discuss the feelings that are affecting his teaching. The response by the principal conveyed positive regard and genuine concern as he reached for Joe's feelings. This same skill could be used to reach for a teacher's feelings on many other issues as well.

When the use of a new technique offers both promise of growth and fear of the unknown, the principal may reach for the fears to help the teacher verbalize them. This process helps to draw out the emotions that may otherwise remain hidden. Such emotions may be far more dangerous when they are allowed to remain below the surface. Above the surface, both the teacher and the principal can face the need to respond to the situation and work toward resolution.

Acknowledging Teachers' Feelings

The principal's skill in acknowledging teachers' feelings is as important in effective supervision as the ability to understand them. The means by which teachers know that the principal understands their feelings is through his acknowledgement. One of the most difficult challenges of this skill is the ability to acknowledge feelings that the principal may not believe are warranted in the situation for the teacher. This requires a degree of understanding that goes beyond the principal him/herself. The fact may be that a teacher should not have rejecting feelings for a particular child but the problem does occur. In such situations if the principal is judgmental as he acknowledges the feelings of the teacher, he may also reject the teacher as the child was rejected. The first step in any effort to solve such problems must be real "value-free" communication of the issues involved between teacher and principal. In some cases teachers may not realize the effects of the feelings they have toward children.

In the example with the teacher who fell asleep at his desk, the principal attempted to acknowledge the feelings involved as follows:

Teacher: This has been the toughest time of my life, there are days when I just don't want to come to work at all.

Principal: You have every right to feel that way, this has really hurt you deeply hasn't it?

The principal thus conveys understanding and acceptance of the feelings that are involved. Joe went on to explain that he had absolutely no warning that his wife was leaving him. They had what he thought was a good relationship. The principal listened as Joe explained the depth of his sorrow. The principal then began to explore sources that the teacher could turn to for help and the implications of the situation on his teaching ability. Although dealing with marital problems is not part of the role, providing assistance, referrals, and dealing with the impact of personal problems on the work are appropriate functions for the principal.

Putting Teachers' Feelings into Words

There are situations when teachers may stop just short of verbalizing their feelings. Fear, anxiety, uncertainty, and many other factors may cause them to behave in this way. The skill of putting teachers' feelings into words is used by the principal when such circumstances arise. In the previous example the principal sensed the reluctance on Joe's part to seek help. The principal tried to articulate the feelings:

Principal: You seem pensive now. Are you concerned about asking for help?

Teacher: I'm afraid that this whole thing will become a topic for discussion and I can't face everyone knowing the whole story.

Principal: Only you can make the decision to seek help, but what has happened to you could happen to anyone. The important thing is that you get the kind of help you need so that you don't have to face it alone. The reason I'm involved in this discussion is that your personal situation is related to the recent problems with your teaching and we need to talk about them.

Teacher: This thing has hit me very hard. I find it difficult to think about anything else. At night I can't sleep and in the morning I can't get up for work.

Principal: I can surely understand how difficult it must be for you. However, I'm concerned about your work with students and particularly their reactions to events in class. I have a number of complaints about needless repetition of material and unruly behavior. This is not easy to say, but I also have perceived some signs that you are drinking during the day. These are signals that you may also be having a problem with alcohol, perhaps related to your stress. These were never problems for you in the past. Can we iron out these issues and keep your classes on an even keel?

Teacher: Drinking is not a problem! I just haven't been concentrating on my teaching duties and I've let work slide a bit. I don't feel good about that and I want to deal with it.

The principal's concern for both the personal situation and the classroom implications was reflected in his empathic responses. The path to the teaching problems was made through concern for the teacher's well-being. If the principal had begun the conference with a direct assault on the complaints about his teaching, he may have encountered hostility and defensive reactions. Some defensiveness may have emerged in relation to the drinking where denial is usually high. At this point, the principal can only monitor the alcohol issue. However, it was important to raise it. In addition, the decision to seek personal help was left entirely up to the teacher but the principal maintained his responsibility to hold the teacher accountable for his work in the classroom.

The blend of support through articulation of the teacher's feelings and demand for accountability in the classroom is evidence of the principal's supervisory skills. Joe agreed to seek help and to refocus upon improving his work in the classroom. They agreed to meet the following week to reassess the situation.

Skills in Sharing Own Feelings

As previously discussed, the belief that the principal must be cold, detached, and clinical is antithetical to the interactional process suggested here. Sharing one's own feelings is an important skill for the principal because it helps him/her to deal honestly with both the supportive and demanding aspects of teacher supervision. The importance of how the principal's feelings are shared cannot be underestimated. Unfortunately, the paradigms of practice for most professionals have incorporated a model which separates the "personal self" from the "professional self." In effect, we are told to leave our personal selves at home when we go to work. The personal-professional split is an artificial dichotomy which leads supervisors to cut themselves off from their most important tool — their own affect. In reality, most of our professional lives is spent learning how to better synthesize our personal and professional selves rather than separating them.

Sensitivity and honesty in this process may accomplish purpose without aggression or hostility, which are likely to be unproductive in the long run. The ability to share his/her own feelings may help teachers to see the principal as a real person instead of a stereotypical role figure. Research in the helping professions indicates support for this notion (Carkhuff, 1971), (Shulman, 1978, 1982, 1991).

Consider the principal who had all the answers to situations or who almost totally lacked affect. The probability of teachers being able to relate to such a person would seem remote. In addition, the expectation for the relationship between teachers and children is antithetical to such insensitivity. It is the ability of the teacher to incorporate both supportive and demanding behaviors in the teacher-student relationship, and to integrate the personal and professional selves that enables children to grow. The behavior of the principal must offer teachers a model of similar sensitivity if the goals of supervision are to be realized.

Showing Vulnerability with Teachers

The importance of bringing the emotions, feelings, and concerns of teachers into the open for honest discussion, thus freeing them to focus their energy on other issues, is paralleled in the behavior of the principal. The capacity to empathize with teachers may be significantly blunted by holding back an honest, spontaneous expression of feelings by the principal. The expression of such feelings offers the opportunity for release and subsequent refocus of energy needed to empathize with teachers.

Vulnerability may be one of the more difficult feelings for the principal to share with teachers. If the principal views his/her role as a "take charge" type leader, he/she may view sharing feelings of vulnerability as a sign of weakness. This position may stem from an unbalanced perception of the dimensions of support and demand in the role of the principal.

Consider the example of the principal who was strongly attacked by his teachers for not voicing serious objections when the superintendent explained a new policy on homework at a district-wide meeting. At a subsequent building faculty meeting, teachers expressed their anger with the principal as he sat there passively accepting the hurt he felt over their attack. He held his feelings, thinking that he would respond less emotionally if he "let the dust settle." This example places the principal in a situation which says that teachers should tell him how they feel in honest terms but he should not be candid with them.

The principal felt that he had not leveled with the teachers and he decided to let them know the following day when he called a faculty meeting. He began by telling them that he felt that they were unfair in the way they attacked him yesterday over the meeting with the superintendent. He explained that he argued for staff supported changes in the policy during the draft stages at the school board meetings. No purpose would be served by him attacking the superintendent in front of the entire district faculty and they should have understood that. There are times when teachers should be upset with him but clearly this was not one of them.

A long silence followed the remarks by the principal and then a discussion began in which the teachers admitted that they made the principal the object for misplaced aggression. Their real anger was with the board for what they felt was insensitivity in the writing of a policy that they had to live with. They went on to express their feeling that the district had no appreciation for the effort and difficulties that teachers faced in working with children in the classroom. After mutual acknowledgement of feelings, they went on to discuss the possibilities for future action on the homework policy. This is an example of the way teachers make the principal feel the same things they do by a process of projecting their feelings on him. Thus, when the principal is made to feel defensive and insecure, the root cause may lie in the defensive and insecure feelings of teachers. This is an example of one of the many parallels that exist in the school environment.

By ignoring or suppressing her/his feelings, the principal is cut off from an important tool for enhancing the communication process. By using his/her feelings professionally, the principal can model an important skill for teachers. For example, a teacher may be made to feel defensive by a parent who feels defensive about her/his part in a child's school problems.

Showing Anger with Teachers

Anger is an emotion that poses a different kind of problem for the principal. In addition to being difficult to express, anger generates negative feelings that make people back away. The open expression of anger by the principal brings with it the danger of a break in real communications and the loss of the relationship needed to work effectively with teachers. Negative feedback expressed inappropriately offers a serious risk in potential loss of relationship. The appropriate expression of anger never treats others inhumanely or impugns their dignity. Negative feedback must assert the objection with no accompanying attack on the person for whom it is intended.

The difficulty in holding anger back is that the feelings remain and they can block effort and energy needed elsewhere. Apathy, antipathy, and depression may all be encouraged by withholding the expression of anger. Appropriate expression of anger is vital to both teachers and the principal if they are to work together effectively. One may seriously question whether supervision work is being accomplished if neither teachers nor the principal ever experience anger with each other. An effective supervisory relationship requires a good deal of pushing and pulling which insures a certain amount of anger.

Concern over the expression of anger is that it may be used inappropriately. Because of the differential power between a principal and a teacher, this is a real issue. The solution which suggested that a supervisor never get angry is not realistic and it leads to more indirect expressions of anger couched in professional terms. For example, a principal who confronts a negative teacher and asks her/him "How long have you had a problem with authority?" is angry. Only the way anger is expressed makes it much more difficult for the staff member to deal with it. Since the staff member is very likely to recognize the anger anyway, it may be more constructive to express it directly.

The key to the constructive use of anger is for the principal to consider where the anger is coming from. If the anger is related to the faculty making the principal feel that he/she is not doing a good job, it probably will not be helpful. If it is misplaced anger directed at the staff because of the pressures the principal is experiencing, it will be destructive rather than positive in effect. In cases such as these, it is more important for the principal to take responsibility for his/her behavior and apologize. If anger is rooted in the principal's genuine caring about the faculty and students, it may be just the confrontation needed to get people moving. Anger from someone in authority who has taken the time to build a fund of positive relationship is often experienced as caring.

In reality, most principals suppress their anger because they are afraid it may evoke an angry response from teachers. Very few principals find the thought of facing an angry teacher or faculty an enjoyable prospect. However, if the principal is doing his/her job correctly, there should be times that staff is angry because the principal has confronted them when they needed it. If the faculty is never angry at the principal, there is probably a problem of lack of expectations. If the teaching staff is constantly angry with the principal, there is a fundamental problem with the relationship.

Figure 5.0 lists some of the additional obstacles in the work phase. Contextual considerations and action strategies are also given.

Figure 5.0
ADDITIONAL OBSTACLES IN THE WORK PHASE

OBSTACLES	CONTEXTUAL	ACTION STRATEGIES
Communication difficulties	Anxiety regarding role differences Lack of clear understanding of teacher concerns	Elaboration cluster —moving from general to specific —containment
Generality	May convey underlying ambivalence	—focused listening
Inadequate listening	Often questions belie real concerns: —emotions mask true message —projection of fears	—questioning —reach inside silences
Confrontation of difficult issues	Questions may help avoid defensive/aggressive stances	
Silences	Silences always carry a message —sign of passive anger —often evoke defensiveness	
Pressures of teaching	Complaints from parents Paperwork Budget constraints	Empathic cluster
Principal's perception of authority	Myth that familiarity must be avoided	Judicious blend of demand & support
Productivity problems	Teachers' feelings; family/school stressors	Reaching for feelings
Lack of verbal- ization	Fear, anxiety, uncertainty	Acknowledgeing feelings

Figure 5.0 (continued)
ADDITIONAL OBSTACLES IN THE WORK PHASE

OBSTACLES	CONTEXTUAL	ACTION STRATEGIES
Communication breakdown	Viewed by staff as detached	Skills of sharing feelings; Model for sensitivity; Offer refocus of energy; Show vulner- ability
Impact: holding back anger, blocks energy/effort	Anger generates negative feelings if personalized	Negative feedback must assert the objection without personal attack
	Appropriate expression of anger is vital for effective work	

Chapter 6

THE DEMAND FOR WORK
WITH TEACHERS IN THE MIDDLE PHASE

THE DEMAND FOR WORK

So far, the model of the work phase of teacher supervision emphasized the importance of dealing with feelings. It began with the principal tuning-in and using the supervisory skills of empathy and elaboration to develop a working contract which incorporates teachers' concerns. This can be viewed as a form of "demand for work." The principal seeks to make the work real by insisting that it be invested with affect. Despite efforts to cultivate an open, honest, and real relationship between the principal and teachers, it is likely that a point will come when ambivalence, and possibly resistance, will arise. It is at this point when the principal's skill in making another type of demand for work is appropriate. This consists of a facilitative confrontation.

Testimony to the difficulty and complexity involved in resistance to change in schools is widely available in the literature (Fullan, 1982), (Goodlad & Klein, 1970), and (Berman & Mc Laughlin, 1975). With reference to the resistance problem, Joyce (1983) describes homeostatic forces in schools which act to maintain stable patterns of behavior. As the work of supervision proceeds, the principal may find the teaching staff to be both for and against growth. Teachers often will reach toward new and promising endeavors then reach a point where they may resist those endeavors in preference for familiar routines. The supervision techniques suggested here enable teachers to recognize their own contributions to issues, to take responsibility for their actions, and to lower their defenses in solving problems dealing with difficult feelings and subjects. Principals need to understand resistance to change (Gattiker, 1990) and not fear it. Ambivalence and resistance to change among teachers is an inevitable part of the effective supervision work of the principal and the basis for the demand for work.

Understanding the Process of Change

The relationship between safety and growth has been discussed by many authors in the literature on human behavior and organizational development (Maslow, 1954), (Schein, 1968), (Mc Clelland, 1965), (Rogers, 1951). In the words of Maslow (1968, p. 47), "We grow forward when the delights of growth and the anxieties of safety are greater than the anxieties of growth and the delights of safety." Lewin (1951) described a model for change that views the individual personality in a form of balance with the environment, referred to as "quasi-stationary social equilibrium." His view of change requires this balance to be broken. For a teacher who was very defensive, for example, denial of the need to change teaching techniques may represent a means of dealing with painful self-doubt about teaching competency. Albeit, a form of equilibrium is thus maintained, it would probably prohibit growth for that teacher. Lewin sees growth occurring from a confrontation with reality.

Lewin suggested the first step toward change is "unfreezing" this equilibrium. This is followed by a state of "disequilibrium," and, finally, a "refreezing" to a new level of quasi-stationary equilibrium (Singh, 1990). The defenses which maintain a level of equilibrium are of great psychological value since they become part of the teacher's sense of well-being. The principal should not expect that the process of moving through the three stages with teachers will be quick or easy. The dynamics of the growth process between principal and teachers is an important part of the ultimate outcome. The nature of the difficulty with growth may be that the more serious the issue which change evokes, and the more deeply the teacher feels it as a threat to the self, the more guarded and ambivalent about change he/she will be.

From Lewin and others cited above, important implications may be drawn for the principal in his/her supervision work with teachers. First, expressions of ambivalence and resistance from teachers must be regarded as indications of normal, healthy behavior and not as acts of aggression against the principal. The principal should not fall victim to the self-fulfilling prophesy of meeting hostility with hostility, or that is likely to happen. A principal who never encounters teacher resistance may not be expecting enough from his staff.

The literature on safety needs suggests that teachers need to feel secure and be supported by the principal if they are to abandon the safety of convention and try to implement new techniques. Joyce suggests (Brandt, 1987) that for many teachers "... it's coming out of that box and for the first time getting some sense of whether they are any good or not." He goes on to say that principals need to be part therapists. In another context, Joyce and Showers (1982) suggest that early attempts to incorporate new skills are likely to be less functional and teachers need to feel good about themselves in order to keep experimenting. The need for empathic skills by the principal is well supported by these suggestions. Further, if the principal is able to understand the feelings which lead to defensiveness and hostility, the resistance side of ambivalence, then he/she is in a much better position to reach for the growth side in a way which may be less threatening to the teacher.

A final implication about growth and change in working with teachers is that the principal may need to make a "demand for work." The implication is that the authority of the principal may be necessary to urge completion of the contract for growth when ambivalence immobilizes the teacher.

Making the Demand for Work with Teachers

When no movement occurs in the growth process, the expectations of the principal may serve as a source of strength for the teacher. Principals who fail to understand the nature of the growth process with teachers may withdraw at the first sign of resistance. This may be a sign of lack of confidence in their ability to supervise teachers. Understanding the resistance side of ambivalence in such situations may enable the principal to approach the teacher, asking "are you prepared to work together on this?" instead of withdrawing. This posture offers no opportunity for the work to evanesce into obscurity as is the case with many teacher performance objectives written in September, submitted to the central office, and forgotten by all until the final report in June.

The resistance side of ambivalence is surely responsible for what Joyce (1983, 69) refers to when he indicates that in most schools there is a tacit understanding that principals and teachers "not encroach" upon their respective domains. This eliminates the need for confrontation of the ambivalence. When the teachers and the principal agree to such norms, the illusion of work is the only recourse. No real effort toward growth is made or expected by either side despite verbal discussion, meetings, and staff development programs to the contrary. Based upon the literature on change in education (Fullan, 1982), this may be a fairly common phenomenon. If growth among teachers is to be accomplished, the principal must understand the process and he/she must have the courage to play the necessary part that effective supervision calls for by refusing to be put off by efforts to lower expectations.

It may be exactly when teachers try to reduce expectations for growth that they may be closest to accomplishing it. The strength of the principal's expectations for their completion of the work may be all that is necessary for real growth to be realized. The ability to understand the meaning of such emotions is what Combs (1971, p. 190) refers to as "reading behavior backwards." The ability of the principal to blend supportive and demanding aspects of their supervision role must be done individually, each in his/her own way.

The demand for work is not restricted to a single facet of supervision, rather it pervades the entire process. When the principal engages in the process of contracting, he/she is making a demand for work. Even the effort to bring teachers' feelings into focus is a form of a demand for work. When coupled with empathic responses, the demand for work is gentle. It may also be confrontive when events and circumstances suggest that it is necessary for the principal to do so.

Facilitative Confrontation: Facing the Truth Together

When confrontation is necessary, the principal must approach the teacher in a supportive manner. Research in the helping professions (Carkhuff, 1969) suggests that this is an important skill in encouraging movement. The need for such confrontation is often brought on by persistent inattention from a teacher to aspects of teaching that are neglected or that fall short of expectations. The need for intervention by the principal may be masked by an effort on the part of the teacher to suggest that no help is necessary. It is also important to note that such confrontation may require the principal to violate social norms described by Joyce (1983, 68) and incur negative social pressures from the staff. Facilitative confrontation may be a vital key to movement with teachers in many situations. It is a supervisory skill the principal must have in his repertoire.

Partializing the Teacher's Concerns

Often when circumstances seem overwhelming in working with an individual teacher, a number of interrelated issues make it difficult to focus on any one thing. Helplessness is a common perception in such situations with the teacher feeling immobilized and not knowing where to begin. Partializing is an essential problem-solving skill that the principal may use to divide a problem into component parts and help a teacher address one part at a time. Task analysis is a similar skill used to divide subject matter into component teaching objectives. Both of these help to develop smaller more manageable chunks of information. The skill of partializing is illustrated in the following example. When a long-term substitute was hired in the middle of a school year for a teacher who was seriously ill, and would be out the rest of the year, she reported to the principal at the end of the first day looking distressed and upset. She proceeded to complain:

Teacher: Filling in for Mrs. Olson is no easy task. She has no lesson plans for me to work with. I have almost no clue about where she is with her classes. The students tell me a different story with each period. I guess she just jumped around in the text with each of her classes in no planned order.

Principal: Sounds like you need to be pretty careful about your diagnosis of each class. How do you plan to proceed?

Teacher: I am not comfortable jumping around in the text but I'm not sure just what to do at this point.

Principal: Let's begin by examining the curriculum and the grade syllabus for each of the different levels in your classes.

Teacher: That may help generally, but how do I know where to begin?

Principal: Using the syllabus, curriculum, and the text, we need to put together a diagnostic test for each level.

Teacher: That is an excellent place to begin. Will you look them over and help me decide on the items?

Principal: Let's meet Wednesday and I'll have the department head help us as well.

Although partializing did not solve this problem, it was an effective means for developing a departure point. The principal helped the teacher to break the problem down to smaller parts and take the first step in the process of solving the problem. The effect here was to reduce the substitute teacher's anxiety and to involve the principal in working with her to begin the supervision relationship on the right track.

Holding the Focus

Often when conferences with teachers cover a rich field of information, movement from one issue to the next can be ineffective. The danger in such cases is that the discussion goes so rapidly that no real growth or meaning is derived from the interaction. Holding the focus tells the teacher that the principal intends to treat the issues carefully and to discuss them thoroughly.

Checking for Underlying Ambivalence

One of the dangers that the principal faces is that teachers may give the appearance of agreement while feeling ambivalent about an idea or proposed change. Teachers may not want to confront the principal with their feelings, leaving him/her unaware of the teacher's true doubts. The principal, in turn, may not want to encourage doubt so he/she makes no effort to reach for it to bring it out in the open. The ultimate effect is that both principal and teacher may be participating in the illusion of work with no real movement toward growth occurring.

It is important to note that the principal, in trying to avoid bringing doubt into the open, may actually have encouraged it to flourish. Only when doubts and ambivalence in such situations are fully explored and discussed do they lose their power and leave teachers free to act. What is suggested for the principal in such situations is that he/she listen carefully, understand and respond empathically to the ambivalence, and demand that teachers act in spite of their reluctance. The principal must not be too quick to accept agreement from the teacher. Rather, he/she must check for underlying ambivalence from the teacher.

Challenging the Illusion of Work

Since the illusion of work is often the path of least resistance, it is easy to fall victim to it. The supervision process in such schools often finds the principal and teachers engaged in conversations about school improvement or professional growth which have little or no meaning. As described previously by Joyce (1982), resistance to change and sanctions directed at the principal may encourage the illusion of work. He refers to these as homeostatic forces operating to maintain the status quo in schools. It is essential that the principal call attention to this situation as the first step in dealing with it. In some cases, principals may be reluctant to confront such circumstances because they are part of the illusion. Uncertainty about how to foster growth and development may encourage principals to avoid direct confrontation of the illusion of work.

An example of challenging the illusion of work by the principal in an individual supervision context deals with passive resistance in the teacher's response. A kindergarten teacher who believed in an almost entirely affective approach with her students, had a student who read well and needed out-of-grade placement for reading and math. At the end of the first week of school the principal met with the teacher to discuss the mother's request for placement in a first grade reading group. The kindergarten teacher agreed that it was appropriate for the child to be placed in the first grade for two subjects and remain with his peers for socialization purposes in the rest of the curriculum.

A month had passed when Mrs. Hayden, the boy's mother, called the school to ask when the first grade placement would be made. She insisted that her son was bored by the lack of a challenge with the kindergarten material. The principal called the teacher into his office to discuss the situation:

Principal: We need to talk about the Hayden boy.

Teacher: He is quite happy in my class.

Principal: We agreed that he was to be placed in the first grade, and you were to have made the arrangement some time ago.

Teacher: I wanted to give him time to adjust to school before moving him up. I will do it soon.

Principal: That is the same answer you gave me two weeks ago when I asked you about him. I get the feeling that you find it easier to put this off than to deal with it and I don't think that you are being honest with me.

Teacher: Frankly, I worry about his ability to relate to first grade children. Oh yes, he can read, but he is not mature enough to deal with those children.

Principal: That's better! Now lets talk about how we can handle the situation and what resources and alternatives we should consider.

In calling attention to the teacher's pattern of resistance, the principal gave her notice that evasion of the issue was no longer acceptable. Simultaneously, the teacher was encouraged to begin explaining what she really felt, rather than what the principal may have wanted to hear about the issue. If the teacher had evaded issues similarly in the past, the principal may need to discuss the way she had learned to deal with people in authority. Such a discussion would be directed toward the development of a new supervision relationship which revises the teacher's way of relating to the principal. When the principal identifies the illusion of work, a critical first step is taken in helping teachers develop a new culture for teaching which encourages honest efforts toward professional growth and staff development. Figure 6.0 offers action strategies for two obstacles which suggest a demand for work, resistance, and unsatisfactory performance.

Figure 6.0
RESISTANCE TO WORK AND
UNSATISFACTORY PERFORMANCE

OBSTACLE	CONTEXTUAL CONSIDERATION	ACTION STRATEGIES
Resistance to work	Ambivalence/resistance to change Tacit understanding in schools not to encroach on respective domains	Understand process of change Demand for work Refuse to lower expectations
Unsatisfactory performance	Staff often claim no help is needed Violation of social norms Feelings of helplessness Tendency to cover too much ground Meaningless rhetoric	Facilitative confrontation Partialize teacher concerns Hold the focus Check for underlying ambivalence Challenge illusion of work

Chapter 7

THE PRINCIPAL'S ROLE
IN DEALING WITH OBSTACLES

The model of the work phase of teacher supervision described in the previous chapters is, by design, a simplistic reflection of the realities of the daily interactions of the principal. For purposes of explanation, the elements and skills in the model are presented as conceptually independent when, in reality, they are phenomenally interactive. There is a good deal of overlap in the clusters as well. Challenging the illusion of work could also be considered as an obstacle to growth, making it relevant to this section as well. Examples of previous sections may also be as relevant here. A few cultural factors, however, appear to warrant specific attention. The principal must be mindful of the cultural prohibitions against open discussion of such factors as dependency, authority, income, death, and anger. Depending on social, economic, and ethnic factors, there may be some value and attitude issues which are school-specific. Principals and staff should become aware of the implications of such factors in dealing with students and parents. Society encourages us to behave in certain approved ways in these areas. The difficulty with the expression of anger was touched upon earlier. The problem of dealing with authority is a very real part of the daily interaction of the principal with teachers.

Authority is an ongoing issue which requires clarification and maintenance through open, honest confrontation of the issues. Difficulties and stresses related to the authority should be anticipated, much like the previous discussion on ambivalence. The principal must encourage open discussion of the related problems of authority in order to prevent the buildup of antipathy under the surface of regular discussion. Principals who feel inadequate may interpret authority problems as negative reflections of their abilities. This may lead to a suppression of the related problems instead of confrontation.

Since suppression of the discussion of authority problems is both a cultural and a group norm (Joyce, 1982), the principal must teach the staff to treat him/her as a real person and not a stereotypical symbol of authority. The goal of this effort by the principal is to create a climate in which all feelings related to their work can be openly and freely discussed. If this effort is not made or if it is unsuccessful, the likelihood of negative feelings going underground and emerging later as reductions in effort or morale, increases. Among the effects may be the illusion of work toward growth and/or lower productivity in some form.

When the principal tells teachers that she/he wants the truth about their feelings regarding how he/she is doing the job, he/she must be prepared to hear their responses. Preparation for this requires that the principal think hard about the probable defensive reaction to teachers' comments. If teachers do level with the principal and find a defensive retort for every comment that they offer, they will quickly conclude that the offer was not genuine and further comments are futile. Since this would probably have an adverse effect on the supervision relationship, great care to avoid defensive behavior must be made by the principal.

Teachers may have heard similar offers from a previous principal and their experiences suggest taking a wait and see posture. Teachers may also test the principal by making a few negative comments to gauge his/her reactions. If they are encouraged and they feel that the principal can handle it, they may bring more significant data to such discussions. Conversely, if they are attacked for their remarks, efforts to communicate on the authority theme will cease. It is important to note that the outcome of each encounter between the principal and the teachers on the authority theme will set the tone for the next.

There are a number of subissues of the authority theme which are relevant to the supervisor/teacher relationship. In the course of a working relationship, the implications of role, position as an outsider, supportive function, limitations, and demand function must be given attention.

The Role of the Principal

Given the myriad of responsibilities which the principal assumes over time, this factor is a crucial one which requires a good deal of discussion during the process of relationship building. Depending on the staff member's experiences, the principal may or may not be perceived as a collaborator. Historically, the role of the principal has been a confusing one. With each new staff member the guidelines must be established. Both parties must agree on the role which each will assume.

The Principal as an Outsider

Even if the principal were a former teacher on the very staff which he/she now supervises, after he takes the job, he loses touch to some degree with what teachers go through in working with children everyday. It is well for the principal to understand that teachers may feel he is an outsider regardless of his previous experiences. Recognition of this by the principal is likely to help this situation.

The Supportive Function of the Principal

Norms and conventions against dependency aside, most teachers prefer to have the support of their principal. Because ambivalence may require teachers to send mixed messages about this issue to the principal, occasional efforts to discuss it openly are useful. The relevant generalization which pertains to this issue is that the greater the extent to which the principal provides support to teachers, the greater will be their willingness to accept demands made on them for growth and development.

The Demanding Function of the Principal

The demanding function of the principal, by the nature of its effect on teachers, must involve some negative feelings. The view of such feelings presented here is that they are a natural part of the process of growth. The principal must recognize the danger of allowing antipathy to build under the surface of the regular channels of communication. If the negative feelings are regarded as signs that the work of growth is going well, and regular opportunities to express them is provided, significant deterrents to accomplishment may be avoided. The goal of discussion of the authority theme is not tranquility but honesty. Frank expressions of the real feelings of both principal and teachers is healthy and functional.

Skill in Sharing Data

Sharing data (facts, values, beliefs, etc.) is an extremely important skill in supervision work with teachers. Sources of data are a consideration in the process, as the more relevant the data to the teacher, the more significance it may have. School districts throughout the country have invested considerable effort in providing data on effective teaching to teachers but specific changes in the classroom from such efforts are hard to define. Only when teachers see the importance of specific data will it affect them. Principals may attribute great importance to data but the teachers must recognize its relevance to their teaching/learning situation for that data to have meaning to them. In sharing data, principals must read the subtle cues teachers give when responding. This section explains three skills the principal uses in sharing data with teachers: providing relevant data, monitoring the growth process, and providing data in a way that is open to challenge.

Providing Relevant Data to Teachers

The skill of providing data to teachers requires that the principal have a detailed knowledge of the background and pedagogical skill level of the teacher. Principals must insure that they neither overwhelm teachers with too much data nor oversimplify their focus thus failing to adequately challenge teachers. Careful monitoring through the actual observation of instruction is absolutely essential to the data sharing and growth process. Only through such observation is the principal knowledgeable enough to share data which his observations suggest is relevant to a particular teacher. Teacher responses to the data and the discussion with the principal must be entirely context based. To do otherwise is to ask teachers to consider techniques that may be useful at some future date. This strategy is unwise unless required by lack of other alternatives. In order for teachers to really profit from data sharing, practice must follow the sharing process.

Monitoring The Growth Process With Teachers

The actual process of data sharing must be carefully monitored for cues from teachers in response to the data. This effort is to insure that teachers understand the data and the implications it holds for classroom practice. It is very important that those implications be discussed thoroughly so that teachers' real feelings about the utility of the data is clear. The principal must insure that follow-up procedures regarding teaching practice modifications are completed. Changes in teaching practice are seldom derived through discussion only. The hard work of trial and error with students in the classroom is usually required as a foundation for such changes.

The role of the principal in monitoring the efforts of teachers to develop and refine their teaching skills is perhaps his/her most important task. Sharing data derived from classroom observations is one of the most important factors in fostering teacher growth. The principal must be prepared for teachers, in postobservation sessions and at staff meetings, to sit quietly and continue to nod in agreement when in reality they may have lost some or all of the threads of comprehension. Monitoring insures that this situation will not go unattended. Teachers may not want to show that they do not understand and thus will allow the meeting to continue as though they do. Past experiences in which not understanding was not a problem, as no follow-up steps by the principal were forthcoming, will encourage teachers to assume the same conditions are present now. The principal must use a variety of techniques to monitor the growth process including questions about how teachers see the classroom effects of the data and actual observation of instruction is essential.

Presenting Data in a Way Open to Challenge

Unless teachers feel free to dispute data shared by the principal, he/she may never know how they feel about its value. Principals, who become defensive when teachers are not as impressed with data as they think they should be, encourage teachers to not tell the truth. Such circumstances often lead to the complete lack of implementation of the data in the classroom. Principals must be sure that they understand the differences between their own view of reality and that of the teachers. Sharing the opinions of experts in the field is simply not an adequate means of insuring growth through data sharing with teachers.

It is important that the principal distinguish his own view. Using such phrases as " . . . in my view," or "there are differences of opinion on this," may help teachers to reflect upon the reality of their teaching without an emotional challenge in retort. When the principal presents data to teachers dogmatically, teachers may feel the need to challenge, thus beginning a battle of wills. Principals should be more concerned when no challenge to data is offered by teachers. No challenge to data by teachers may lead to the illusion of work. The principal should invite critical reactions from teachers from the very beginning of the supervisory relationship using such phrases as: "I want you to be direct with me about your feelings on this." Unless the principal reaches for the ambivalent feelings of teachers, bringing them into open discussion, they are likely to emerge as the failure to implement an idea at some future point.

Sessional Ending Skills

The dynamics of sessional endings with teachers require special supervisory skills to insure that the work of the session is not lost. This is the point at which the principal concentrates on how the work of the session will get done. If the session with teachers results in no resolution, the status of the discussion should be focused upon in order to clarify what the discussion covered. The skills which are useful in sessional endings are: summarizing, generalizing, and identifying next steps.

The principal, in using the skill of summarizing, devotes the last ten minutes of a session to a review of the encounter. Any agreements or understandings that have been made with the teachers are restated for mutual clarification. This skill is not an automatic ending to every meeting but a tool to be used at critical moments.

The skill of generalizing is used by the principal to help the teacher or group of teachers to move from a specific situation or issue to a general principal which is relevant to it. Several cases in which children are grade retained may have a common generalization relevant to all future cases.

In all sessions the question of what follows is an important phase. Are specific responsibilities fixed, or should they be, is the focus for this skill. Identifying next steps is a vital skill to insure continued staff participation in real terms. Teachers are not likely to continue to openly discuss and work toward growth if the principal does not insure that their work is in fact carried out. When the principal asks teachers to focus on the next steps, he/she is also likely to uncover any residual ambivalence. This presents another opportunity to complete the work using the real feelings and opinions of the teachers. Figure 7.0 lists some frequent obstacles relevant to this chapter. Contextual considerations and action strategies are also suggested.

Figure 7.0
FREQUENT OBSTACLES

OBSTACLE	CONTEXTUAL CONSIDERATIONS	ACTION STRATEGIES
Misperception of Principal's role	Perception dependent on experience	Supportive function preferred
	Often seen as outsider Demanding function will normally create negative feelings	Frank expression of real feelings from both sides
Staff not given feedback	Information regarded as meaningless if importance is not translated/made explicit	Data must be relevant to classroom
	Data is without value when staff not involved in the process	Data presented in a way open to challenge
Lack of progress	Focus on how work of the session will get done	Sessional Ending Skills —summarizing —generalizing —identifying next steps

Chapter 8

PROMOTING GROWTH WITH INDIVIDUAL TEACHERS: THE ORIENTATION AND PREOBSERVATION SESSIONS

The skills required by the school supervisor in the promotion of professional growth with individual teachers is the focus of this section. This function is extremely important because growth in teaching skills translates directly into improved learning opportunities for children. The object of this effort is the development and refinement of the teaching skills of individual teachers. The process involves a collaborative effort in which the principal and the teacher analyze the process of teaching, reinforcing, refining, and remediating from pedagogical, curricular, and interactive bases. The ultimate goal of this process is for the individual teacher to take charge of his/her professional growth (Glickman & Gordon, 1987). It is the focus upon the individual teacher in this supervision function which distinguishes it from the role of the principal in working with teachers as a group.

This chapter recognizes the individual and unique qualities associated with teaching practice and the need for personalizing instructional supervision (June et al., 1987). It views the teacher as the primary decision maker in the growth process and it incorporates techniques which enable the supervisor to deal appropriately with resistance and ambiguity in the process of change. The principal must employ interactive skills which incorporate both supportive and demanding behaviors in the process of supervision to accomplish meaningful growth with individual teachers. In exploring the role of the principal in promoting growth with individual teachers, this chapter defines some of the important assumptions which support the process. It then applies the model presented in earlier chapters to examples with individual teachers.

Supporting Assumptions

If the teaching and learning process in promoting professional growth were a matter of transmitting important information, growth and change in public schools would be simple. The immense difficulties in the process of promoting teacher professional growth and change are well documented (Goodlad & Klein, 1970), (Berman & McLaughlin, 1975), and (Fullan, 1982). In the early 1970s the initial notion was that all that was necessary to develop teachers were consultants who knew their subject matter and who had the ability to transmit it. This myth was subsequently modified to incorporate some degree of participation by the teachers in the process of selection. Both of these methods persist today in the programs offered by school districts for teachers. A fatal flaw in them is that most are externally experienced by the individual teacher. Seldom does internalization of methodology occur without practice and ongoing evaluation. The teacher may be acted upon by many external forces but the power to act is internal. Support for this contention is offered by Blumberg and Jonas (1987, 58) when they describe a teacher pretending to listen with no intention of acting on the suggestions of the principal.

Neither the school district nor the principal should regard the teacher as a passive object onto which ideas may be projected. While most supervisors would likely agree with this position, inservice programs in many school districts are simply one time exposures to a myriad of methodologies. Ironically, many of the very programs that see the teacher in this passive role may be extolling the need and virtues of active participation in the classroom as part of an effective teaching program.

The central assumption in this chapter is that the promotion of growth among teachers is an extremely personalized and highly individualized activity. The unique aspects of personality that become part of teaching style require that professional growth be derived through personal experience and that for change to be lasting, it must be meaningful to the individual teacher. The feelings and beliefs of the individual teacher are an extremely important part of the process. The implication here is that teachers change because they want to and not because the principal or anyone else wants them to. The principal and the teacher are partners in the professional growth process, sharing in the emotions and ideas that result (Blumberg and Jonas, 24).

The principal must recognize the idiosyncratic nature of teaching and the fact that meaningful growth requires active re-creation of the teaching segment/process by the teacher. Attempting to tell the teacher what to do, avoiding the active re-creating process of self-discovery, is not likely to produce lasting change. The principal can be a central resource but the development of the idea, understanding, or generalization must be undertaken by the teacher. The principal must focus upon the interaction between the ideas to be implemented and the teacher, monitoring feelings, beliefs, and behaviors. It is in this sense that the role of the principal is much like a mediator in the process of promoting growth with individual teachers. Effective supervision involves continuous movement between specific analysis of the teachers thinking, beliefs, and intentions and the generalizations which emerge from observed classroom practice.

Another assumption in the process of growth is that teachers must be encouraged to practice new skills and try new ideas in the classroom. Implicit in this assumption is that refining new teaching techniques may require numerous efforts which are less positive in their impact on children than the original practice. Teachers must feel free to experiment with new techniques without fear of recrimination or the possibility of poor results. This means the principal must permit and encourage teachers to make their own mistakes. He/she must also assure teachers that the investment of such effort is well worth the increased understanding that results even when the effects may be mildly discouraging. The principal must provide support for these efforts so that teachers will keep trying to develop and refine their skills.

Figure 8.0 shows the elements included and the definition of professional growth used in this chapter. Commitment means the willingness to invest considerable effort in the process of modifying teaching techniques. The expenditure of such effort must be sincere as the illusion of work is an ever present temptation in which no real commitment is made or expected in implementing ideas generated in the analysis of a lesson. Personal and professional change is viewed here as possible for anyone with adequate commitment to support the process. Commitment is an ongoing concern which must be periodically raised by the principal and carefully checked to insure that the teacher is genuinely comfortable with the process and the current direction which it is taking.

Understanding is an equally important but more concrete ingredient in the growth process. The general direction of the process is the reduction of the discrepancy between actual classroom practice and the theory-

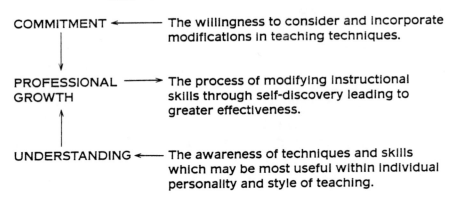

Figure 8.0
ELEMENTS OF PROFESSIONAL GROWTH

COMMITMENT ←——— The willingness to consider and incorporate modifications in teaching techniques.

PROFESSIONAL ——→ The process of modifying instructional
GROWTH skills through self-discovery leading to greater effectiveness.

UNDERSTANDING ←—— The awareness of techniques and skills which may be most useful within individual personality and style of teaching.

based suggestions. Since the theory base is subject to great individual interpretation, no specific formula or recipe is useful to the principal. The principal must however have internalized the general principles of effective teaching in order to provide useful feedback to teachers in the analysis of teaching. Teachers must also have a strong theory base either from undergraduate preparation, from inservice training or both. Such training is not intended to provide a recipe which must be followed but rather a set of elements from which a lesson may be formed, taught, and subsequently analyzed. The effective teaching research provides support for lesson analysis and a common vocabulary to facilitate discussion. Research suggested conclusions are not to be religiously adhered to as laws but rather they serve as a guide to support analysis, encourage consideration of alternatives and stimulate discussion. The teacher is the primary decision maker who selects the particular combination of elements to be included in a lesson. Understanding is a major goal of the post lesson analysis and conference between the principal and the teacher.

Decisions in the act of teaching can be made intuitively or consciously. Intuitive teaching decisions may be as effective as those made consciously but they are seldom chosen from a field of alternatives for their potential value over other alternatives. They are unconscious choices which may always be convenient but are hard to analyze for their value in increasing the teacher's understanding of the act of teaching. Understanding is increased as teachers rely less on intuitive and more on conscious choices in instructional decision making.

Reflective collaboration, enabling teachers to consciously choose intervention strategies from his/her interpretation of particular circumstances and relevant theory, can be an effective technique to refine practice. Reflective teaching involves the conscious selection of choices which are derived through analysis of theory and the dynamics/results of past and present experiences in the classroom. It is a means of developing self-critical, ever evolving, and self-reliant teachers. This task is accomplished through continually reestablishing relationships between observed classroom teaching practice and the teacher's understanding of the thinking and the relevant generalizations which emerge from the analysis of that practice. This effort insures individual relevance for each teacher yet builds bridges of understanding based on a common theory base among all teachers. It also encourages individual diversity in the interpretation of that base. Reflective collaboration is a primary means through which the principal and teacher may facilitate professional growth. The objective of reflection is to help the teacher understand the implications and results of his/her thinking as it is reflected in the instructional decisions observed in teaching practice.

Lesson Analysis — Bridges to the Theory Base

Central to the process of promoting teacher growth is the analysis of teaching. It is useful to adopt a framework to analyze teaching which is closely linked to the theory base or the research on effective teaching, and which is well understood by the principal and the teachers.

The supervision techniques suggested here are internally directed. They are intended to work within the individual teacher's thinking, beliefs, intentions, and behaviors. The use of any lens to facilitate discussion and analysis of observed teaching behavior must regard the theory base and any of the models of teaching, such as direct instruction, as resources to encourage and expand thinking discussion and consideration. Great care must be exercised by the supervisor to avoid over generalization and highly prescriptive application of the techniques derived from research data from the theory base to particular teaching situations.

Any lens selected as a framework for lesson analysis should be a means of encouraging discussion and increasing understanding. It should not be viewed or perceived as a formula of required steps in the process of teaching. The literature offers many choices of such tools which are often referred to as lenses through which teaching may be viewed and analyzed (Borich, 1990), (Hunter, 1984), (Acheson and Gall, 1987). The principal should consider lenses which are relevant to the respective content area, mutually useful, and acceptable to the teacher being observed. Flexibility is an essential quality of any such lens which is selected as a means to facilitate lesson analysis.

The lens selected for use in this chapter was adapted from Hunter (1980) and the literature (Berliner, 1984) on direct instruction. It utilizes elements which are well represented in the literature on effective teaching. These elements are not a list of required steps and they may be selected in any combination preferred by the teacher to accomplish the learning objectives of a particular lesson. They also form a common language which helps both teacher and the principal to discuss effects achieved and explore the thinking involved in the selection of the particular combination of elements included in the lesson. The reflective process is used with the elements in the analysis of the lesson with the goal of increasing the understanding of the teacher and thereby making his/her teaching decisions progressively more effective.

A Guide to Lesson Analysis

1. **Lesson Purpose and Objective.** Clarity in the intended outcomes is viewed as an important step in the conscious decision-making process of lesson planning. The purposes of the learning and the objectives (what students were to be expected to learn from the lesson) were understood by the students.

2. **Adequacy of Teacher Input.** The teacher input activities (explanation, modeling, demonstration, and/or any other means used to convey information, meaning, or understanding) provided students with an adequate explanation of content of the lesson.

3. **Clear Examples.** The teacher provided clear examples in sufficient numbers to illustrate the skill, concept, or objective of the lesson.

4. **Monitoring and Adjusting.** The teacher continuously monitored student understanding using techniques which involved many students. Appropriate adjustments were made by the teacher as they were indicated by the responses from students.

5. **Practice Activities.** The teacher included sufficient practice opportunities to provide students with adequate facility to accomplish the learning objective independently.

6. **Closure.** Students were given the opportunity to summarize new learning or review previous learning.

7. **Learning Principles.** The principles of learning (motivation, reinforcement, retention, and transfer) were appropriately represented in the interaction in the class. The atmosphere was positive with an appropriate pace of activities to insure continued interest and involvement by the students.

Formal and Informal Supervision Sessions

The process of individual teacher supervision may include both formal and informal sessions. The formal sessions, often prescribed by policy or contract, are frequently part of a teacher evaluation procedure required by state law. This process is usually more rigorous or at least more frequent for the nontenured teacher during the probationary period. Formal sessions are often scheduled with adequate notice and they are part of a cycle which includes activities and responsibilities for both teacher and the principal. The cycle involves a sequence of sessions shown in Figure 8.1, some of which are repeated in the course of the evaluation period which may be one or more school years.

Informal sessions can be an important source of data through which the principal gains a deeper understanding of the skills of the individual teacher. These sessions are not scheduled or prearranged but rather take place spontaneously. The principal or supervisor walks through the building entering classrooms for brief periods of five to ten minutes (Natriello, 1988). This practice becomes easily tolerated by teachers and students as it is used more frequently. Soon no notice is made of the presence or movement of the supervisor and lessons continue as if no observer were present. When this technique is carefully connected with positive reinforcement of effective teaching practice, teachers often begin to accept and welcome the observer (Giandomenico, 1988). Reinforcement may be most effective in written form such as a note which cites a specific teaching behavior that positively affected students with the reasons for the affects and a suggestion for continued use of the practice. Such notes may be accumulated in teachers' files providing them with written affirmation of their observed skills. This technique encourages teachers to develop confidence in their own ability and it supports a constructive and trusting relationship with the supervisor.

Supervisors often ask about circumstances in the informal observation where serious concerns arise in the lesson. The supervisor in this situation should continue to observe for a longer period of time to collect sufficient data to support a postobservation session with the teacher. Rarely will this situation occur as a complete surprise to the active principal or supervisor. When it does he/she must not treat the situation casually but rather attempt to deal with it in the most appropriate manner possible. Such a session should focus directly on the behaviors which triggered the deep concerns of the supervisor. The remainder of this chapter will explain each of the formal supervision sessions and provide examples of typical school cases to demonstrate the sessional skills defined in earlier chapters.

Figure 8.1
THE SUPERVISION CYCLE

I.   The Orientation Session
II.   The Preobservation Session
(The Lesson Observation)
(Presession Planning)
III.   The Postobservation Session
IV.   The Summary Evaluation Session

Formal Supervision Sessions: I. The Orientation Session

The orientation sessions for individual teachers should be supported by one or more large group discussions in which the principal clarifies his role in supervision and the purposes of the various sessions. It may be necessary with new teachers to provide orientation sessions without them having been present in the large group discussions. The orientation session is designed to provide a broad understanding of the process/procedures that will be followed and to reduce teacher anxiety by providing relevant information and a supportive stance. The content of the orientation session is derived from the building operational procedures, classroom practice, the individual teachers concerns, and the supervision role established by the principal. The process techniques used by the principal are the preliminary and beginning phase skills described in earlier chapters. The following examples illustrate the skills applied to orientation sessions with a beginning teacher and with a veteran of ten years experience in the classroom. The modulation of supportive and demanding behaviors is a critical skill which the principal must manage appropriately to insure growth is realized for each teacher.

The Beginning Teacher

The beginning teacher in the following example has just completed undergraduate training and has no significant experience to rely upon in starting with a class of children at the beginning of the school year. The curriculum, school procedures, and many other issues may be overwhelming. The principal must be careful not to increase the teacher's anxiety needlessly with a large amount of less than critical information. Including in the required reading in such cases the history of the school, the minutes if the faculty meetings for the past two years, and the Board policy manual may be examples of relevant but less critical information.

New teachers often may be fearful about the probationary process and the principal in general. Helping them to overcome anxiety is a first step in building a trusting relationship that will enable the principal to provide support in critical areas involving classroom skills. Most new teachers are fearful about telling the principal the areas in which they are having difficulty. Such admissions may be seen by them as working against their acquisition of tenure. The principal must convince the new teacher that problems are normal and expected. Open and honest communication are more likely develop between the teacher and the principal when the teacher begins to develop confidence that such admissions lead to solutions without danger of recrimination. When professional growth occurs through such collaboration with the principal and the individual teacher is credited with self-accomplishment, the foundation is made for the development of a self-critical, analytical, and self-efficacious teacher.

In the following example, John, the principal of Millard Elementary School, hired Nina, a beginning first grade teacher, during the summer and they agreed to meet before school started to discuss mutual concerns about the first weeks of school. The orientation session begins with John welcoming her to the school.

Principal: I want to welcome you to our school and the community. We are fortunate to have a dedicated staff and supportive parents. I noticed you have put a great deal of effort into preparing your classroom. It looks just great. I am pleased that you are going to be teaching in our school.

Teacher: I am also pleased to be here. I like the building and my room in particular. The access to the media center from my room is a real plus and I hope to use it to great advantage after we get underway.

Principal: The purpose for our meeting today is to provide you with information on some of the key areas of operation to make your first days of school as smooth as possible. I want to give you an opportunity to ask questions and to share your concerns first so we are sure to talk about them. Would you like to begin by touching upon one or two of the things that you have been wondering about? For example, new teachers are often concerned about the type of support and supervision they can expect. Questions about the schedule are another example.

I brought a teacher handbook which will give you the schedule and the building routine. It may answer many but probably not all of your questions. As we get closer to opening day, you will have different questions and I hope you bring them to me as they arise. I want you to feel comfortable doing that. The teachers all meet together for lunch breaks so don't be concerned about feeling isolated.

Teacher: Now that you mention some things, I've heard that this school expects teachers to be highly effective. Do you have these expectations for first year teachers as well?

Principal: One of the strengths of this school is that we have high expectations for teachers, and in turn, for our students. However, you are just starting out in your teaching career which is both an exciting and difficult time for you. We don't expect you to have everything worked out but rather we see this first year, and your future years here as a kind of learning process. You will have time to learn and you will be able to make mistakes along the way. It's rather like a puzzle that works on all of your professional life. Some parts of the puzzle fit easily and others are more difficult. All teachers go through this learning process. I will try to help you discover what works for you.

Teacher: How does the actual process work?

Principal: My job is to help you to look at your own teaching. The first weeks of school are normally difficult for new teachers until routines are established with the children. It's my job to help you to do that. After you get started, we will look at areas of your teaching to develop and refine your skills. We will work at this together with you trying various strategies and me observing and providing feedback. We will discuss alternatives and work together to refine your skills. We will work through a cycle of observation, discussion, and revision of technique. Then the process will be repeated. My job is to provide support to you and if I fail to do that adequately, don't let me get away with it. I want you to feel free to ask for help when you need it, from me, or from your colleagues. I will try to be available to listen when things seem to be rough. Together we can overcome anything that comes up, so don't worry, we are a team. Remember, this is a process and you are not expected to start out with the skills of a seasoned veteran.

A discussion followed which led to management strategies that helped to insure a good first week of school for Nina. John stopped by after school to see how she felt on the first day. Nina thanked him for helping her to think through a management system. She felt that it was time well spent. John used informal supervision techniques to maintain his supportive relationship with Nina until a formal observation could be comfortably arranged. John was careful not to overwhelm Nina with too many expectations on several fronts. Rather he tried to be sure that she was in control of her classes from the very beginning of the year.

The Experienced Teacher

Experienced teachers may be as apprehensive about supervision as new teachers but may act as if no anxiety exists. Symptoms of anxiety may appear indirectly. The experienced teacher has also worked with at least one other supervisor and has very likely formed attitudes, feelings, and opinions about the value of supervision. These may be obstacles to the present relationship and they must be explored and neutralized. The experienced teacher may be just as unlikely to be candid with the supervisor if in previous experience, he/she viewed such behavior as reducing anxiety or avoiding the need to confront unpleasant circumstances. In the following example, a veteran teacher feels that no assistance by the principal is needed or desired. Maureen, the principal, is greeting Peter, a fifth grade teacher, as their meeting begins.

Principal: I'm glad we arranged to meet this week in spite of our busy schedules. I wanted to discuss the supervision process to be sure that we understood what to expect from each other.

Teacher: I'm not sure what you mean. I understand that you will be evaluating me but why do we need to discuss it? Why don't you observe me and then tell me where you think I need to improve? After all these years I don't really think I will need much help.

Principal: I was hoping that we might help each other. You've been here a long time and you are familiar with the curriculum. Maybe we can share ideas about methods which have proven successful.

Teacher: I understand that you have to evaluate me and I must participate, but I don't see how this is a benefit to anyone; as a matter of fact it may be a waste of our time since we both have much to do.

Principal: I'm grateful to have you level with me. As long as we remain open with each other, I feel that we can talk honestly. I don't want this process to be a waste of time for either of us. But that makes both of us responsible for deciding how to use the time effectively. I feel a deep responsibility to understand what's going on in all of the classrooms in the building. Frankly, I feel that all of you teachers should demand nothing less for me as principal. Can you fill me in on how the evaluation process was conducted in the past?

Teacher: The principal would observe each of us and then write a report which we cosigned and forwarded to the central office. They were happy and so were we. No time was wasted in unnecessary meetings.

Principal: Since you began teaching in that situation and then taught for ten years, it doesn't surprise me that you are concerned about how this process will effect you. You have every right to feel unsure about your willingness to participate in this process with me.

Teacher: I just don't see how this will make me a better teacher.

Principal: Let's talk about how the process could work and then see if we can agree on how you feel it would be most helpful to you. My role with experienced teachers is more like a consultant, another set of eyes, and another view point from which to discuss what we see in your classes. I see you taking much of the lead around our agenda for discussion. I am not here to tell you what to do or how to do it. But there is a responsibility that I must fulfill in the process which is required by law. I would like to try to fulfill that role meaningfully and with the best interests of children in mind.

Teacher: Exactly what do you see us doing in this process?

Principal: We will talk about your teaching and record examples of effective strategies. We will discuss your thinking, and the effects achieved in your teaching decisions. We will consider the potential effects of various alternatives and select some that are acceptable to you. As you incorporate the selected behaviors into your work with children, I will observe and provide feedback on your teaching. This process is collaborative with a mutual commitment to growth required by both of us. I have heard that you are an excellent teacher and I hope to gain some insights from you. Are you willing to give the process a chance to work for you?

Teacher: Suppose we can't agree on things as we discuss my work? How do we resolve our differences?

Principal: We will discuss the situation fully to find out where and how we disagree. In most cases, you are free to use or not use my ideas. Only in those situations where I feel a serious problem exists or I am required to make a final decision will I insist. I see this essentially as a collaborative process. I think we should let the process unfold and take one step at a time. Will you try to work together and see if the process can be useful?

Teacher: I'm not sure I'm ready for it, but I'll try.

In this example the principal tuned in to the teacher's previous experience and found the root of the problem. No previous positive supervision experience has left the teacher feeling that certain risks are involved in the process. The principal responded empathically, suggesting that they should give the process a chance to work for them. The process was clarified when the principal explained how the procedure would work. As the process unfolds the principal may need to clarify and insure that the contract is understood again.

In both orientation sessions the principal connected with the feelings of the teachers and then clarified the procedure hoping to encourage a commitment. The process may be more directive with a beginning teacher where the first experiences with children are critical to the establishment of a functional teacher/student relationship. Care was taken to be sure that a management system was organized in preparation for the first day of school with the beginning teacher. Yet the teacher was given approval to make mistakes. The experienced teacher required clarification to overcome previous experiences and anxiety connected with the supervision/consultation process. The principal will need to continue exploration of feelings in future sessions to reveal probable feelings of insecurity which may be masked by resistance.

Formal Supervision Sessions: II. The Preobservation Session

The preobservation session is intended to explore the preactive thinking of the teacher. It also is used to clarify the objectives and the context of the class so that the principal may better understand the teacher's intentions and the lesson to be observed. It affords an opportunity to narrow the focus of the observation and where appropriate, to refine the data collected. The preobservation session is not required in all situations.

When the principal has worked with a group of teachers for a number of years and the process is familiar to everyone, a preobservation session may not be necessary. Such judgments may be best left to the principal and the particular situation rather than a hard and fast rule requiring one each time a teacher is observed. It is also important to recognize that the narrowing function of the preobservation session may also be achieved through the previous postobservation session.

When the principal is new to the building or when a new teacher is being observed, it may be more helpful to use a preobservation session. In such circumstances the principal may use the opportunity to reduce the teachers anxiety and to discuss areas wherein the teacher has voiced concerns and requested assistance. In the following examples, the preobservation session is used to accomplish these ends.

The Beginning Teacher

During the first two weeks of school John visited informally with Nina to monitor her reactions and feelings in the classroom. She expressed great concern that she was overwhelmed with efforts to diagnose and reach each child. John suggested a formal observation and a discussion to talk more deeply about the situation. They agreed on a date for a preobservation session and Nina is just arriving in John's office as we join them.

Principal: Nina I want to begin by commending you for a number of excellent teaching strategies which I have observed during my walk through visits. You have a very supportive teaching style with children. You seem to know intuitively which of your students will require additional attention. This is a powerful skill and which will be helpful in your teaching.

Teacher: Thanks! Sometimes at the end of the day I wonder if I have done anything right.

Principal: Now let's talk about your concerns. Tell me how you feel things are going with your students.

Teacher: I agree with your comments about my awareness, but I'm worried about reaching all of my students. I feel that some of them are particularly difficult to reach and I'm never sure that they understand what we are doing. When I look at their homework, my fears are often confirmed since they seem to be unable to complete the work.

Principal: Can you describe one of the students you are concerned about. Perhaps if we can think through the problem with one student, we may gain some insights we can generalize to the others.

Teacher: Frank is a good example. He sits in class and seems to be understanding what is going on. At least he looks attentive. When I ask if the class understands something I have taught, he nods his head in agreement just like all of the others. Then I see the written work and it's clear that he didn't understand at all.

Principal: You are already demonstrating an important skill—individualizing—in that you are able to observe individual students in the class as well as the class group. I think it is very helpful that you are checking your students' understanding as you teach the lesson. You already know that Frank is not accepting your invitation to tell you that he is not getting it. Let's use a skill that I find helpful which is called "tuning-in." Put yourself in Frank's shoes for a moment and consider why Frank may not be letting you know he is lost when you invite him to respond.

Teacher: Well maybe he is embarrassed to admit he doesn't understand. Maybe he thinks I will consider him dumb.

Principal: Good! That's a start. Is it possible he thinks he is the only one who is not getting it?

Teacher: That's possible but not true. There are some other kids who are also lost.

Principal: But Frank doesn't know that. What are some other possible reasons for his not completing the homework?

Teacher: Well, sometimes he comes into class looking sleepy in the morning and he is usually not dressed well. I asked him about it once and he told me that he had not had any breakfast that morning. I'm not sure anyone is paying attention to him at home.

Principal: You may be on to something. A number of our kids are living under difficult circumstances ranging from abuse and neglect on one end of the continuum to not having any privacy in their homes to study. There may be some home-related factors associated with Frank's difficulty and when combined with his unwillingness to admit that he is not understanding, may be making him fall more and more behind.

Teacher: If that's so, he must be feeling miserable. That would make it even harder to learn.

Principal: Nice! You have really tuned in to Frank.

Teacher: You know I'm so nervous about being a new teacher, I just assumed I was missing some kids because of the way I was teaching. I didn't really think about their difficulties in learning.

Principal: I actually like that quality in you as long as you don't over-emphasize it. Many teachers feel defensive about their teaching and are quick to blame a breakdown in the learning process on their students. You are open to looking at your part in the process which is an important stance to take for your future professional growth. Would it help if I observed a class and focused on the children who seem to become lost and on what points in the lesson they seem to lose it? We could talk about the way you taught the lesson, but also, about how to handle the class conversation when you sense people are lost. If you feel comfortable, we could use the videotape recorder to give both of us a chance to focus on particular class issues.

Teacher: I think an observation session might be helpful.

Principal: You give me some times when you would like me to observe and I will check my schedule. Now, let's not lose Frank and the other kids that you are concerned about. Did you ever talk directly to Frank about the problem?

Teacher: Yes I did.

Principal: What did you say to him?

Teacher: I told him I had reviewed his homework and I felt he was not completing it. I asked him if he had problems with the material, and he said he was sorry and he would try to do better.

Principal: What were you thinking and feeling when he said that and what did you say back?

Teacher: I was frustrated because I knew he was having problems understanding the material but he wasn't admitting it. I didn't say anything and just hoped he might do better. But things haven't changed.

Principal: I think it's hard for some of our children to believe anyone really cares about them. You were reaching out for Frank with genuine concern for him but he may have heard your comment as being critical. When we back off immediately, I think our kids are not sure we are really interested. What would have happened if you had trusted your instincts and stayed with it. For example if you said something like this: "I know you want to do well Frank and that you are trying hard. But sometimes things can get in the way. I wonder if you have any help at home with homework or if you even have a place of your own where you can work quietly?"

Teacher: I like that response. I don't think he would hear criticism because I said he really wanted to learn. Perhaps if I give the examples, the way you did, he might open up a bit. Maybe I need to follow-up with his mother on parents' night.

Principal: Nice! Your starting to think about individualizing. If it turns out to be a bigger problem, we can ask the school social worker to do some further work with the family. As part of the conversation you might also open the question of his getting lost in class and not admitting it when you ask.

Teacher: I could ask him if he thinks he is the only one getting lost and let him know he is not the only one. Perhaps I can work out a signal with him so he can let me know if he is not understanding without feeling embarrassed.

Principal: Not only would that help, but you may need to talk to your whole class about the general issue of what to do when some students feel lost—both how important and how difficult it is to ask questions. The general discussion may also help Frank. Most important to him, I think, is that if you continue to reach out, he may not feel so alone and hopeless. You have just done some excellent work on individualizing which you can apply to the other students you are concerned about. Maybe we can talk about them a bit next time and see how things went with Frank.

In this case, John, the principal, tuned in to Nina's feelings of anxiety while at the same time providing her with some options for diagnostic/corrective action. He began by crediting her for effective teaching techniques. This beginning relationship building strategy enabled the teacher to establish initial trust. It parallels the process in which she is going to credit the student for really wanting to learn. Thus she began to reveal concerns about her adequacy in working with children. This set the stage for initial contracting to evolve. The principal began with a manageable intervention strategy. This effort is likely to develop her investment in the process since improvements are apt to increase her feelings of efficacy.

The principal also introduced many ideas about individualization of children in class and a recognition of the complexity of the teaching-learning process. The teacher's immediate assumption that some children not learning was related to her presentation was challenged, but done so in a way which credited her willingness to examine her own work. The principal also started using a valuable tool called "memory work." He asked the teacher to describe some of her conversation with Frank from memory. She was re-creating her intervention, including at the Principal's request, her feeling and observations. It is through the re-creation of specific conversations with children and teaching interventions that the principal will get a better sense of the process and an opportunity to help. The analysis of the conversation was handled with support for the teacher and as a collaborative process. After moving from the general discussion of children not learning to the specific case of Frank, the principal asked the teacher to reverse the process and to generalize her insights to her work with other such children. The offer of the videotape process for further work was politely declined by suggesting the observation process. As the working relationship grows and the teacher's confidence in herself and the principal increases, the principal can return to discuss videotaping as a threatening, but valuable tool.

The example above illustrates how the principal can combine process and content goals into supervision procedures. It takes only a small degree of speculation to forecast the course which this interaction may have taken were the principal not sensitive to the dynamics of the situation.

In the second case we turn to Paul, an experienced teacher, who was reluctant to invest in the process. We join the session as Paul and John begin the preobservation discussion.

The Experienced Teacher

Principal: I'm glad we have the chance to talk before I observe your class tomorrow. I want to get an understanding of where you are with the class and what I will be seeing. Since the orientation session, have you given any thought to how this process might benefit us?

Teacher: Not really. I've been very busy. Look, I'm a good teacher and I'm not sure how this will help.

Principal: Hold on a minute. I'm trying to do some observation and supervision work with all of the teachers in the school, not just you. It doesn't mean I don't think you are a good teacher.

Teacher: Look I've been around. We have had principals before who came in and make changes like this to try to look good. The word is out that you are here to clean out some of the experienced teachers.

Principal: That's simply not true! I know it may take some time to trust me, but the fact is that I am impressed with the faculty thus far and I would like to hold on to veteran teachers like yourself. I realize that introducing a new procedure such as observation is going to generate some mistrust and resistance. However, I think even the best teachers need to keep on growing in their work or they get stale. Also, I have an obligation to become familiar with your work and observation is one way to do it. I'd like to approach this in a cooperative manner since I know this is the only way it is going to be helpful. My hope is that after we work together you may start to trust me and realize I have no hidden agenda. I'd like you to think it over and let's talk about it again on Wednesday.

Teacher: I'll do that (still sounding angry).

In this preobservation session the principal is confronted with a number of obstacles: stalled communications, mistrust, and strained relationships. He first tried to reassure the teacher by generalizing the observation process. Then he began to explore more sensitively the contextual issues which he perceived to be operating. Problems with authority, fear of revealing inadequacies, and work avoidance appeared to be potential factors. In addition, the principal made a demand for work by the teacher in the process while indicating a willingness to give the teacher time to reflect. Again, the underlying process issues are far more important than the surface issues associated with the evaluation procedures. It is unlikely that any real work would have been accomplished if these issues were not neutralized. It is still possible that the teacher may erect barriers to put the principal off and delay the observation. While the principal needs to respect the defenses to allow time for them to lower, it is important that the principal conveys the message that in one way or the another, the process will be implemented. If the teacher does not respond, then other means of evaluation and documentation are open to the principal. This type of situation is not uncommon. Other results in similar situations may be stalled communications and/or the principal giving in to teacher pressure by a tacit agreement to avoid mutual encroachment on the other's domain.

The process whereby these underlying concerns are identified, acknowledged, and acted upon may enable the kind of professional skill development which many administrators claim to be seeking. This chapter focused on the orientation and preobservation sessions. The next chapter will focus on the postobservation session. This session is the most frequently used and powerful session of all. It is thus accorded a complete chapter to more adequately explore its potential and to provide robust examples of the process skills developed in the earlier chapters.

Chapter 9

PROMOTING GROWTH WITH INDIVIDUAL TEACHERS: THE POST OBSERVATION SESSION

The post observation session is perhaps the most powerful tool available to principals and teachers in the pursuit of teaching skill development/improvement. The goal of the session is to improve teaching skills and to strengthen the teacher's beliefs in his/her ability to achieve instructional objectives with children. Depending on the teacher's capability and experience, the process can vary from supervisor-directed to entirely collaborative in nature. All of the variation between these parameters is possible and typical.

The principal initially may capitalize on his/her expertise in directing the lesson analysis/objective-setting process, particularly with new teachers. This may be followed by a gradual shift toward teacher self-directed analysis. Because the process necessitates a close working relationship and direct involvement of the principal in the entire teaching process, teachers are made to feel that their efforts are not going unnoticed. This support from the principal serves to minimize feelings of isolation often experienced by teachers. Using the previously discussed interaction skills, principals help teachers to expand their instructional thinking.

During the post observation session a collaborative effort between the principal and the teacher evolves. The post observation session is used to elucidate the relationship between intended and actual results through analysis of teaching segments. It affords the opportunity for the principal and the teacher to discuss the effects of teaching decisions and alternatives thereby increasing their repertoires. It encourages self-awareness and appropriate redirection of teaching practices. The post observation session is the aegis through which reflection and teacher growth is achieved. It is repeated in a sequence designed to connect lesson observations in a cycle and to identify patterns. This avoids the tendency to view each lesson as an individual snapshot in preference for a more sequential and complete picture of the skills of the teacher. Connecting observations is accomplished through the development of objectives derived from each session which frame the next observation. A narrow focus is thus achieved for each succeeding observation and the refinement process continues through refocusing on additional behaviors and thinking of the teacher in each session. The use of written objectives helps the principal and the teacher to avoid trading one set of instructional symptoms for another in successive observations.

Objectives Derived from the Post Observation Session

Three types of objectives are developed from the post observation session: reinforcement, refinement, and growth. Reinforcement objectives reinforce effective practice. Refinement objectives are developed to extend existing practice and growth objectives are directed at the development of additional practice skills. All of these objectives are developed at the post observation session using a systematic process that encourages the participants to consciously associate behavioral principles with lesson segments. If the process of setting these objectives is carefully developed by the principal, with meaningful involvement of the teacher, real growth is a reasonable expectation. Such involvement may be an eventual goal in the situation of a beginning teacher with little experience or an immediate objective with a veteran. Refinement and growth objectives from one post observation session eventually become reinforcement objectives for the next observation, thus linking observations together.

Collecting and Sharing Lesson Observation Data

Prior to the actual post observation session, the principal must observe the lesson and collect data to be shared with the teacher. If possible, the teacher should also be given the opportunity to see and analyze a videotape of the lesson. One of the most important skills in the teacher supervision process is gathering data through lesson observation. The skill of sharing data in a way open to challenge was discussed in chapter seven. Collecting data in the observation of teaching requires a commitment to objectivity. Data collected should be descriptive not judgmental. The data and the means used to share it must not discourage the teacher's efforts to form revisions through reflection. The principal may be tempted to see, through his/her own experience, the flaws in the presentation of a lesson. Such reactions must be placed aside in order to allow the teacher to make and learn from his/her own mistakes. This fosters the development of a self-critical teacher. In the pursuit of such a teacher, the task of the principal is to modulate supportive and demanding behaviors appropriately in order to foster growth with individual teachers. The data collected from the observation of teaching is a powerful tool which the principal uses to help the teacher explore and reflect on the thinking, decisions, and effects achieved with students in lessons.

The usefulness of the data gathered in an observation may be increased if the principal uses the preobservation or a previous observation session to refine the focus. When such a narrowed focus is well understood, the teacher's investment in the data increases and refinements are more likely to be attempted and incorporated. It helps the teacher's internal process of reflection to direct growth with less external reliance on the principal.

Analysis of the Observation Data

The principal uses some form of note-taking to record the behaviors from the observation. The notes may be in rough form with numerous shorthand techniques used to record a large amount of teaching decisions/ behaviors in a short period of time. The notes may be improved if they are reinforced quickly by memory. This means improving them by using recall soon after the observation is completed. With a good set of notes, the process of analysis is greatly improved. Notes which are either inaccurate or incomplete may be a detriment to an effective session.

Analysis of the data is accomplished by overlaying the elements of effective teaching (from the agreed upon guide to lesson analysis) on the events in the lesson. This effort seeks to determine which elements were present and how they contributed to the accomplishment of the objectives of the lesson. The analysis also considers which elements are missing and the potential contribution they may have made to the lesson. The post observation session is intended to focus upon the teacher's rationale for the behaviors observed. The first step is to insure that the behaviors in the lesson are well documented by the principal, enabling him to help the teacher to uncover his/her thinking. The analysis should provide the participants with an indication of the teacher's strengths, needs, and trends.

Planning and Strategy for the Session

In preparing for the session the principal must form a plan that he/she may use as a guide in working with the teacher. The plan is quite tentative and it may be modified as circumstances suggest. The plan helps the principal to be prepared for the discussion with potential questions and it enables her/him to have a better perspective on the eventual outcomes that may be achieved in the session. The plan should include areas of reinforcement, refinement, and growth which are well represented in the documentation. The edited notes from the observation and the analysis are also included in the plan. Other issues which the principal may wish to consider in developing the plan include the frequency and significance (effects on the behavior of the children) of teaching behaviors observed. Individual qualities of the teacher such as the capacity, level of understanding, comprehension limits, and experience should also be considered. Great care must be taken never to disparage the teacher.

The principal must also examine his/her own motives, fears, and anxiety. Preparing questions and examples from notes is useful, particularly when first developing the process skills used with teachers in the post observation session.

Conducting the Post Observation Session

One goal of the post observation session is to help to develop and refine the teacher's understanding of the relationship between his/her thinking, beliefs, and actual classroom behaviors. A second goal is to help the teacher deepen her/his understanding of the interaction in the class and its impact on the achievement of the learning objectives. These are accomplished through the discussion and analysis of observed teaching practice. In the outline below, the sequence, content, and process implications of the post observation session are represented:

CONTENT = What	PROCESS = How
Beginning;	
Introduction	Tune-in, based on preparatory empathy
orientation	sense feelings, reach for them
outline	articulate and acknowledge feelings, empathic skills
Middle;	

Explore thinking	Elaboration skills
discussion of	Data-sharing skills
intentions, actions	Contracting skills
results	Demand for work

Ending:

Agreed-upon areas	Sessional ending skills
for reinforcement,	Summarizing
refinement, and	Generalizing
growth.	Identifying next steps

Post Observation Session

The Beginning Teacher

The first years of a teacher's career are crucial to the development of professional skills. Depending on the nature of the undergraduate experience, new teachers enter the classroom with diverse sets of skills. The principal should be sensitive to the concerns, feelings, and circumstances that surround each new staff member. It is helpful if the principal begins to consciously employ the skills of tuning in early in the process so that assumptions are not made which may create obstacles to relationship building. The preobservation and post observation sessions represent the first formal interaction between the principal and the teacher and sets the stage for the kind of relationship that will develop. Anxiety can be high for both the teacher and the principal. Both may be harboring fears of insecurity regarding expectations, roles, and capabilities. Accordingly, principals and supervisors must be cautious about process implications while focusing on content issues of instructional skills of new teachers. Principals must be cognizant that new teachers are going to need help with a number of interactions such as faculty, parents, students, building routines, etc., during the first weeks of the school year. These factors should be considered so that supervisory demands will be within reason and excessive information is not allowed to overload the first-year teacher.

Lesson analysis provides the principal and teacher with a vehicle for examining the implications of a myriad of professional skills. However, without careful modulation of demands, the process can become overwhelming. It is incumbent on the principal to regularly assure the teacher that the supervisor has a good command of lesson design/analysis skills, communication skills, curriculum expertise, and learning theory.

We join a post observation with Nina in November, three months into her first year of teaching.

Principal: Nina, can you believe three months have passed since you've begun? I was so pleased yesterday to see your class relating to you. It's obvious that they respect you and look to you for direction.

Let's review a bit how far you've come before we get into developing some growth objectives. I know how overwhelmed new teachers can get when they're in the midst of their first year. Unless they step back and gauge progress, it may feel like nothing's being accomplished. When you were concerned about the students' understanding, you agreed to start looking at the issues of difficulty, pace, and information processing. During each subsequent lesson observation conference we've been able to tease out these components and document your work on them. Is this aspect becoming any easier for you?

Teacher: It's finally starting to jell. When I plan a lesson now I'm able to judge how to reach the objective by applying the questions we've developed during our sessions. Actually, it's becoming a challenge rather than a problem now.

Supervisor: That's great! I am definitely seeing evidence of these gains when I observe your classes. Nina, yesterday it was apparent that you invested extraordinary effort and time into lesson design. It seems like the materials you used for an anticipatory set must have taken you hours to create.

Teacher: I want to be an excellent teacher. It takes time, but I think it's worth the effort.

Supervisor: You've become ill and needed to go home several times. Could you be pushing yourself too hard?

Teacher: Oh, I don't think so. I've been picking up viruses from the children. I'm usually fine by the next day.

Supervisor: Have you considered that maybe you have to look at the expectations that you have for yourself a little more closely and maybe be more realistic about how much investment specific tasks should take?

Teacher: (Silence)

Supervisor: I'm not being critical. I'd hate to see such a competent beginner burn herself out before the year's end.

Teacher: I don't think I will, but I'll sleep on it. I do have very high expectations for myself.

Supervisor: Nina, Let's get back to yesterday's lesson. How would you describe it using the process we've been practicing the past several weeks.

Teacher: I really liked the beginning of it. I understand the components of the anticipatory set and have fun figuring out ways to make that section interesting for students. And I'm getting used to clarifying the objective so that students know what's going to be accomplished in the lesson.

Supervisor: I agree with you. Your idea to create an analogy between alphabet soup and compound words was very effective. The children were very invested in the task and participated actively.

Do you think we're ready to move on to another phase of lesson design?

Teacher: It's finally starting to make sense for me. Let's move on. . . .

Analysis

Nina, a bright articulate young woman, is extremely receptive to learning intervention techniques and to analyzing her lessons. She uses the supervisory relationship very effectively. The principal's observations of her zealous commitment (documented by classroom appearance, lesson preparation, and involvement of countless hours beyond the regular day) caused him to select this area for exploration. She appeared not yet ready to explore the implications of her behavior. However, as their relationship develops the principal would likely return to this process issue as it pertains to implications for job performance. Administrators run the risk of treading on clinical issues in some situations. They must remain cognizant of their limitations yet confident enough to deal with situation which have potential professional implications.

The Experienced Teacher

Tom and Jerry taught side by side for years in the seventh grade. When Jerry was appointed principal the entire faculty expressed the typical amount of ambivalence associated with being happy about the appointment, yet apprehensive about the role/authority implications. In Tom's case the feelings were intense as he wrestled with the new relationship.

Principal: I scheduled an appointment with you because I feel we really need to talk about how things have changed for us and to see if we can resolve some of the issues.

Tom: I don't know what you're talking about.

Principal: We used to be best buddies. Now all I feel is tension between us. You walk out of the teachers' room when I walk in. At last week's faculty meeting you and Judy chatted during the entire session. You seem to be going through the motions, but I sense you're angry.

Tom: You've come in with so many demands. Remember how we used to laugh and joke around. . . . ; now you're playing the game.

Principal: I knew you were going to say that. I've been trying so hard to figure out my role. I keep weighing the issues of control with being a softee. It's so tough. When my best friends become so distant, however, it really tears me up.

I worked hard the last couple of years to develop some skills of supervision. I think I can work together with you guys if you'll meet me half way.

Tom: I think we've both been avoiding discussion. You know the teachers think you're swaggering around like a central office lackey. We thought we were bad off with Charlie as principal; at least he left us alone.

Principal: Is that what you want from a supervisor? We complained for years because no direction was given from above. There must be a way to work this out even though it won't be easy.

Tom: How can you possibly help me? I was here before you and taught you everything I know. I get so angry when I have to come in here and act as a subordinate just because you have the power of position.

Principal: You're still angry about my appointment. I know how you feel, but I don't agree that we can't work together. Look, the Board has a supervision process. I've done a lot of work trying to adapt it for our use. I can't live with myself if I fold and tell you that it doesn't apply to you.

Can't we work out some expectations for each other? You know I respect your competence and will expect you to be largely self-directed.

I must know, however, how students are progressing and how teachers are fostering that growth. I won't give up my responsibility in that behalf.

Tom: I don't think things will ever be the same between us. You've changed too much.

Principal: I hope you're wrong. Over time, our relationship may be different but I don't want it to be an adversarial one. I'll do everything in my power to avoid that.

Analysis

This session was a painful one and probably only minimal gain was achieved. However, the situation is a common one. The importance of the interaction is that it occurred. The supervisor raised the issues of authority and role conflict and forced them into discussion so that the source of Tom's anger was finally acknowledged. He seemed to be denying these feelings but they were causing him intense discomfort and subsequent passive aggressive tendencies were emerging. Such acknowledgement may eventually diminish its effect.

Jerry confronted the issue of their working relationship and established that he would not relinquish his responsibility as a supervisor. While Tom did not budge, the message was clear that it should be an area that would be dealt with despite resistance. Jerry would not agree to no supervision. A contract offer was clearly made, despite Tom's defensiveness. At this point it is in Tom's hands. Once the obstacle has been surfaced it may lose its power. If not, additional steps may need to be taken to document the refusal of the teacher to accept supervision.

Such changes in relationships are difficult on both sides. Eventually, a delicate balance may be reached; as long as feeling issues are counterbalanced with appropriate demands and expectations.

The Negative Teacher

Nothing is so disconcerting to a classroom as is an atmosphere of negativism. Often teachers who are judgmental in their approach are unaware of the devastating effects it has on children. Since such behavior is often imbedded in a rigidly held value system, the administrator must employ both process and content techniques to help to encourage some self-awareness on the part of the teacher.

This conference is joined midstream after the teacher has been credited for embodying numerous effective teaching techniques into her lesson design.

Principal: Judy, I want to summarize this portion of the conference by reinforcing you for developing a very effective lesson. You motivated the children by developing an exciting anticipatory set. The students were on the edge of their seats in anticipation of the lesson. It's obvious that you have a clear understanding of each youngster's capability in the way that you provided information and asked salient questions. Your models were clear and the amount of practice seemed effective.

I noticed Bobby was having trouble sitting still during the class and wondered how you were experiencing him. He strikes me as a child who could be frustrating to you, particularly when the rest of the class seemed so connected to the work.

Teacher: I'm not sure a child like Bobby belongs in my class. I run a tight ship. I don't allow disobedience. I believe as long as you respond immediately, the whole class falls into line.

Principal: I noticed that the children respond to your authority which must make it even harder with Bobby in your class. What do you mean you don't think he belongs in your class?

Teacher: Look, we both know Bobby has been diagnosed as having an attention deficit disorder. He belongs in a special education class. I would have gone into special education if I wanted to manage behavior all day.

Principal: I realize we have a problem here with the issue of which of these kids need the special education class and which can make it in a regular class. You may be right about the need for a special class and I'd be willing to explore that if we can't get anywhere with Bobby. What I'd like to do is see if I can be of help in terms of the problems he creates for you right now so we can fully determine if he is able to make it or not. For example, would it be of help if we can get a volunteer to spend some time with him during the week to give you moments of peace? We can determine when the most difficult times are and try to arrange some help.

Teacher: Yes! I'd appreciate some relief.

Principal: I was able to concentrate on Bobby during the class, since I didn't have to worry about the lesson, and I made some observations which you may find helpful. Bobby seemed to be most agitated when you took some time to work with another child on an individual basis. I could be wrong, but I began to suspect he wasn't as much just misbehaving or trying to annoy. It may simply have been his way of trying to get your attention. My hunch is that Bobby has developed some maladaptive ways of saying: "I need some help!"

Teacher: Well I can't pay attention to him all of the time. I have a large class and he has to be able to wait his turn and ask for help directly.

Principal: I agree. Perhaps that's where you can be helpful to him. Perhaps you can watch to see if you notice the same pattern, and if you do, you can talk to Bobby about it. If you let him know you realize he is trying to learn and that you would like to help, and that you have to help other children as well, it might make him less anxious. Is there any kind of special signal you can work out with him so that he can let you know when he feels he needs you? Perhaps if he knows you are aware of him, he will not have to keep pushing for attention.

Teacher: I can do that, but realistically, I may not be able to give him enough attention.

Principal: If that's the case, we may then have to call a conference with the team and discuss the possibility of placing him elsewhere. I know you are a good teacher and a class with structure may be just the ticket for Bobby. If he can't handle it, we will need to move him. I'd like to see what happens when we respond to the message he is sending through all of that behavior. Why don't you take a crack at it and we can discuss your observations at the end of the week. In the meantime, I'll see about getting you some immediate help.

Analysis

The principal recognized that this teacher's, at times, rigid behavior in managing her class was a signal to him of her stress. He could hardly ask the teacher to become more attuned to the meaning of the children's behavior if he was not attuned to the meaning of her's. By offering recognition of her stress and some concrete help, he was modeling the very strategies she would have to implement with Bobby. He attempted to join with the teacher by starting from her perspective of the struggle so that she could see the principal as concerned about her as he was about Bobby. Through the work on Bobby, the principal established the idea of identifying patterns of behavior and understanding their meanings, rather than simply attempting to make the behavior disappear. The learning from the work with Bobby can later be generalized to other students in the class and to the class group. This can move the teacher past a reflex response which suggests all spontaneous behavior is "misbehaving." With greater insight into how to handle these different forms of indirect communications from students, the teacher may become less rigid and needing to control.

Chapter 10

WORKING WITH TEACHERS IN STAFF GROUPS

The principal interacts with teachers in both formal and informal staff groups in the work of supervision in a group context. Formal groups may involve grade level, curriculum, or any of a host of other staff group meetings in which teachers come together for school purposes. A significant amount of the principal's time is devoted to dealing with the dynamics of the informal work group(s) which is/are continually in operation as teachers carry out their daily tasks. Ongoing interactions among teachers as they work together are the lifeblood of the informal group. The informal group may develop norms and sanctions which significantly affect the operation of the building and the relationships with the principal. Significant differences in the qualities of the formal and informal groups may be evident within the same faculty. Interactions between the principal and teachers on a one-to-one basis may be positive but when the teachers come together in a group, relations may be constrained by differences which are hidden in the feelings and norms of the informal group.

This chapter will examine techniques which principals and supervisors can use to work with teachers in formal group situations to make them more effective. Issues and problems arising from the unstructured collective of teachers or informal work group are also considered. Examples and issues raised in this chapter were selected because they were frequently raised by practicing supervisors.

For example, an important aspect of teacher supervision involves helping the staff to cope with the working environment. A situation in which the principal finds the staff angry and hostile over a new policy or decision from the central office is not infrequent in schools. Budget reductions, staff layoffs, and other circumstances often find teachers demanding to know on which side the principal stands. The Superintendent may ask the same question. The dilemma of the principal feeling caught in the middle between direction from above and the faculty is an important one in supervision work with teachers.

This chapter begins with general comments about the dynamics of the principal's work with the teaching staff as a group. The potential advantages of open communication fostering mutual support in effective group work is also explored. The questions of principal's role and group purposes are then focused upon in the beginning phase of work with a teaching staff. The development of a supportive group culture, various roles of individuals in the group, and conflict within the group are examined in the work phase of group supervision with teachers. Formal and informal group examples and issues arising from the authority theme are also discussed.

The Dynamics of the Principal's Work with Teachers in Groups

Perhaps deriving from their experiences as teachers with poorly functioning group meetings, principals often express dread and fear with the prospect of group meetings. Some principals feel that teachers often seem different in a group context than in one-to-one interactions. The faculty group takes on a culture that no individual teacher may be willing to break through. After a group meeting when principals ask individual teachers if they agree with the direction taken by the group, they often say: "No, but I could not stand up and disagree with the group."

The possibility exists that the teacher actually did agree with the group, but is having trouble admitting it directly to the principal. In most cases, however, it is safer to assume that silence on the part of group members really means "no" rather than signifying agreement. This is most true when the principal is attempting to gain agreement from teachers on a controversial issue. The natural tendency is to believe that silence means "yes."

Some principals feel that real communication is almost impossible in staff groups. A mutual effort to maintain a superficial relationship may assure that neither supervisor nor teachers face the real issues which may be a source of fear to both. Joyce, Hersh, and McKibbin (1983, 68) describe this relationship as a tacit understanding in which neither teachers nor principal encroach on each other's domain. They go on to describe informal social pressures which are used to enforce such norms. This is an example of the illusion of work where real action is not expected by either side. The rhetoric of both parties is superficial.

Given previous experiences in groups which were unsatisfactory and the distance which often characterizes such relationships, it is small wonder that principals often feel that group meetings should be avoided if possible, or reduced to as few and as short as absolutely necessary. Perhaps where previous experiences are the only basis for practices, principals may know that they are ineffective, but they may lack the skills needed to redirect group meetings into productive channels.

The strength of numbers represented in the size of the faculty group makes it a formidable obstacle for the principal to deal with. Situations in which negative feelings represented in teachers' comments or nonverbal expressions, may make the principal uncomfortable and/or reluctant to explore and possibly face overt hostility. Silences may also arouse the principal's anxiety and tolerating them may be difficult. Perhaps because of their own feelings of inadequacy and fears of being disliked, many principals find work in group situations particularly difficult and unsatisfactory experiences overall. Such practices as leaving difficult issues to the last few minutes of a faculty meeting when little time is available to deal with them, may be indicative of fear of group meetings. Leaving such contentious items for the end of a faculty meeting when little time is left to consider them, assures that reactions and discussion will be superficial. In reality, the strategy of such practices is transparent and teachers very often know that the principal is anxious about the situation. Teachers often continue their adverse reactions in the informal interactions of the lounge where the principal is unable to participate or develop viable action strategies to deal effectively with the situation.

In spite of what may appear to be obstacles, group meetings offer important opportunities to develop faculty support to solve problems and set direction for objectives to accomplish school goals. In order for the faculty to become a potent force to carry out the goals of the school, leadership is necessary to help teachers release their potential for constructive work and learn to function effectively together. The obstacles which emerge in group meetings may be viewed as opportunities to break through superficial discussion to more meaningful communication in which teachers and the principal address real issues and mutual concerns honestly. This kind of development is not likely to happen if the faculty is left to define, address, and implement solutions to problems on their own.

Group meetings, in which the principal routinely reads directives or simply communicates information directly to all teachers simultaneously, often leave teachers wondering why a written memo would not have accomplished the objectives and saved time for everyone. Principals may feel that teachers will not read the memo, but faculty attention may be more illusive at a meeting in which little or no genuine involvement is required. Such meetings often find undercurrents and side conversation as serious competition to the principal. After years of ineffective group meetings, the casual observer to such faculty meetings may find the behavior of both parties to be almost entirely without effect on the other. Teachers talk to each other and the principal simply talks over the informal conversations to everyone with little serious attention given to her/his commentary.

Whenever a meeting of a committee or of the faculty in any form is called, the principal must understand and facilitate the active role of all the teachers in the group process. It may be naive to assume that teachers know how to participate, especially at the beginning phase of a group's development. It may also be naive to assume that, when shown how, teachers will participate easily or willingly in the group. Rather than sitting and waiting patiently for their turn to speak in a meeting, teachers can be actively engaged in the process of listening, if they are shown ways they can be helpful. Teachers will be more likely to respond positively to such participation if they are given both instruction and support as they try to become engaged and regular demands for work are required of them in the group process.

The Mutual Support Process

The Principal must be willing to risk and invest in the effort to make the faculty group effective. The alternatives to such deliberate action are usually easier and less anxiety evoking than squarely facing the illusion of work, with real communication cutting through superficial rhetoric. The prize to be accomplished by this effort is the development of a truly supportive atmosphere of positive group morale within which school goals are defined and accomplished. Faculty apathy, which may be an indicator of underlying problems, can be relieved and teachers' true potential to contribute to school effectiveness may be realized.

An effective faculty group can provide mutual support in many ways. Teachers learn to share data in effective groups and draw on each others ideas, values, and beliefs in ways which are mutually supportive and beneficial. This relieves the principal of the burden of being the only, or primary, source of information. Additionally, the group process offers the opportunity to express and share dissonant points of view, thus freeing teachers to modify and adapt to problems and situations flexibly. When such discord is kept under the surface, resentment and rigidity may develop, impeding open consideration of alternatives and real communication. The effect is to stunt the process of group deliberation, weakening morale and potential for accomplishment.

The group process may be used as a sounding board in which tentative ideas may be offered and adapted as discussion suggests. This process offers expression and discussion in an atmosphere of open, honest, and real communication. Such circumstances offer the foundation for norms in which argument and debate are the basis for a culture for work. Developing the willingness to challenge ideas in a group is not always easy to accomplish with teachers. Suggestions for the development of such a culture with teachers are offered later in this chapter.

One obstacle in the development of a culture for work is the principal. As discussions venture into areas where previous experience is absent or negative, the reactions of the principal are critical. Teachers will watch for a response as a colleague disagrees with the principal. If the first efforts to test the extent of the openness of the relationship between the principal and teachers are met with vehement or defensive objections, teachers may revert to previous experience and hold back honest feelings in preference for superficial rhetoric. The principal must be prepared to live up to promises that he/she can accept criticism openly, respect open communication, and appreciate differences of opinion on all issues. Negative feelings that are not permitted to be voiced openly by the principal will often appear later in the form of poor morale or lack of willingness to participate in school-related functions beyond the classroom.

Mutual support also results from sharing reactions when teachers listen to colleagues explain feelings associated with experiences. Teachers may experience relief knowing that others feel as they do about issues thus making them feel less disconcerting and overwhelming. This has been called the "all in the same boat" phenomenon. They may also discover from such sharing, feelings they were not aware they had. The exchange of empathy in such situations helps to foster feelings of mutual support and respect, which is an important part of a culture for work. New teachers feeling concerned about the reactions of veterans to their occasional outbursts in class to retain control, may be relieved to hear veterans recall similar experiences. Such experiences offer teachers evidence of mutual caring and support as part of a group helping relationship in an effective culture for work.

If the principal cultivates an effective group process, teachers may be able to confront each other with demands as well as support. Peers may be able to make demands on each other more effectively in some circumstances when the principal fosters the proper conditions. When a school policy is adopted by the group and everyone agrees to pull together, teachers often know when someone is not fulfilling the intent of the effort more readily than the principal, who cannot be everywhere as the events of the day develop. In such cases, with the proper foundation, the principal may inquire at a faculty meeting for problems with the new policy. Teachers may address the nonparticipant with questions about how events occurred as they did. When everyone works together for the accomplishment of objectives, such redirection may become possible.

Individual problem solving and rehearsal are strategies which may offer support in group context. A teacher may be apprehensive approaching a hostile parent about a difficult situation, such as the possibility of grade retention. Faculty group members may provide feedback about strategies and procedures as the teacher rehearses the coming meeting. Teachers may welcome opportunities to respond and obtain valuable feedback from their peers on a variety of issues which confront them.

In the following sections the dynamics of the group context in work with teachers are examined and techniques are suggested with examples to illustrate their application. Effective work (the accomplishment of selected directions/problem solving) is possible for teachers on both formal and informal group levels with knowledgeable intervention of the principal and hard work of the faculty.

The Beginning Phase of Working with Teachers in A Group

The beginning phase serves as the foundation on which the principal and teachers build the group's work capacity. The following discussion focuses on the beginning phase of work with a group of teachers in which the principal is newly appointed. Other situations which are particularly relevant to the discussion include newly formed groups or committees or any situation in which the supervisor joins an established group. The discussion is generally relevant to existing groups and supervisory relationships as well. Contracting, the means by which clarity of purpose and of the role of the supervisor is achieved, is the first step in establishing the foundation for future work between the principal and teachers. Whenever groups seem to be floundering, the leader is well advised to use contracting to eliminate ambiguity.

Purposes of Staff Groups

A formal staff group generally consists of a number of teachers who come together specifically to complete one or more school-related tasks. Although it may serve social purposes, staff meetings are primarily intended to deal with school business in some form. Achieving clarity of purpose with such groups avoids the endless meetings in which nothing real is accomplished. Using an appropriate time frame also helps to achieve primary purposes. The temptation to consider interesting but tangential issues is ameliorated by absolute clarity of purpose.

There are many types of group meetings serving school-related purposes. Among the most common are the following: (1) general staff meetings, (2) case collaboration meetings, (3) group supervision meetings, and (4) in-service training meetings. A single meeting may involve more than one purpose. For example, a staff meeting may have an inservice component. When the purposes of each of these meetings is clarified and the role of the principal is resolved, productivity is more likely. This is necessary because the content, dynamics of the group, and focus of the principal differ for each of the different purposes.

General Staff Meetings primarily focus upon the job management aspects of teaching, building operations, matters of policy, and the instructional program. Referred to as faculty meetings, they are often regularly scheduled to discuss and find solutions to daily problems such as better cafeteria supervision or procedures for the use of the school library. Other common issues for these meetings include interpreting administration policies, eliciting reactions, and formulating responses to directions suggested by the central office. These meetings are also used for considering instructional program needs and problems which occur in the daily performance of classroom teaching.

Albeit the principal must develop an agenda for discussion at these meetings, it is important that the faculty have input into the formulation process. One method which may be somewhat cumbersome is to send a tentative agenda to each teacher on the faculty asking for additional items for discussion. This also affords teachers the opportunity to consider the issues to be discussed before the actual meeting. The principal should also begin each meeting tentatively, incorporating sessional contracting skills as explained in Chapter 3. This assures that hidden agenda items are surfaced, preventing resentment from being an obstacle to productivity. If sessional contracting skills are not used, the principal risks the exertion of powerful forces on teachers' feelings which may never be openly discussed or clarified. This condition leads to the illusion of work where both sides talk but never act on issues or objectives.

The following example is a principal's report of how she opened a meeting by describing the agenda and reaching for other concerns of the teachers as discussion items:

"I explained that the new grade retention policy needed to be discussed to insure that we followed the procedures. Parent objections were sure to follow and if the procedures were followed, at least we could rely upon them when objections were raised by parents. I also wanted their input so that I could share it at the next meeting of the administrative council. I then asked them if they had any items that they wanted to add to the agenda. They declined to add to the agenda so I went on with the retention policy. I sensed that they were listening but not hearing and I suspected that something else was on their minds."

In addition to sharing the items to be considered the principal offered the opportunity for teachers to add items to the agenda. It is also important to note that the principal described the purposes for the discussion, to avoid difficulties with parent objections that were sure to come when the policy was implemented. Clarity helps teachers understand the purposes of the discussion and the limits of their discretion on the related issues. Principals should be certain that teachers are not given the impression that they have input into the formulation of policy which has already been agreed to administratively. In such cases, if the teachers decide to pursue a direction inconsistent with established policy, a serious loss of credibility may be inevitable when the principal explains why it is not possible to follow their preference. The principal is well advised to be completely honest with teachers about the limits of discussion, letting them know why their input is sought. It is also useful to articulate the decisions which are made based upon faculty input, and those which are made with faculty input. Clarity in these matters may avoid the accusation of manipulation by the principal, and it helps to insure honest communications.

As mentioned earlier in the chapter, teachers may not be willing participants in the group process. In the excerpt above, the principal invited teachers to add concerns to the agenda and received none. As the meeting continued the principal sensed that the faculty was not participating in the discussion. The principal read the teachers' lack of enthusiasm as a cue to deeper feelings and made a second effort at sessional contracting as follows:

"I noticed a pall had fallen over the room as I explained the retention policy. Knowing the controversy we faced every year with this issue and the lethargy in the room, I asked them if something else was on their minds. Linda responded that the morning paper reported that the School Board intended to eliminate teaching positions to meet finance board demands for reductions in the budget. She added, "we may not have to worry about grade retentions." When I asked if this was their concern they nodded in agreement. I responded "let me fill you in on what I know about the likely areas of reduction and then we can talk about how they may affect you. After that we can return to the retention policy. The faculty agreed and their involvement improved immediately."

There are always important issues to be considered by teachers in staff meetings. One reason that many meetings may be boring is that real agenda issues and concerns of faculty are not discussed but allowed to remain under the surface. Teachers need to be invested in the meeting for it to be effective. Providing an opportunity for them to express the issues about which they feel a sense of urgency is an effective means of increasing their investment in the meeting.

In this example the principal utilized monitoring skills to assess the process of the meeting. When it was apparent that something was troubling the teachers, the principal reached for the obstacle that concerned them. If the principal had missed the cue and assumed that meetings normally operate this way, a valuable opportunity to deal with an issue that troubled many teachers would have been lost.

Clearly, the principal was aware of the tension around the issue before the staff meeting. In many cases, staff will signal the urgency of the issue through an informal comment prior to the meeting. If the principal listens carefully to the "preliminary chatter" which occurs in the room prior to the start of the meeting he/she will often overhear comments hinting at the concern.

Even with advanced knowledge of the issue the principals often omit it from the agenda or leave to the end of the session when there is very little time, if any, to discuss it. The principal's avoidance is often related to his/her own stress around the issue which is not addressed because the principal is unsure where a discussion will lead. Since he/she is usually as much in the dark about what will happen as the staff, there is a reluctance to even address the subject.

This is a mistake since just prior to the announcement of cutbacks or staff layoffs, is one of the points of highest stress for staff in situations such as the one described in the example. The uncertainty itself is one of the greatest stress producers. The principal can be helpful to staff during this time period even if he/she is unsure of what will happen. First, simply sharing whatever information is available, as tentative as it is, helps staff feel that the principal is not "holding out" on them. Second, acknowledging the stress of this time period and allowing staff to discuss it and to provide support to each other is crucial. Teachers can also be asked to address their observations of the impact of the uncertainty on their work. Simply acknowledging the connections between their stress and their teaching can often help teachers to better manage their feelings and cope with their tasks. Finally, if teachers are aware of possible cutbacks and loss of positions, this information is probably out in the community as well. A discussion of the potential impact of this period of tension on students and parents offers the opportunity for teachers to address the professional issues they face in attempting to relate to student and parent concerns while trying to manage their own stress. It is often helpful for teachers to use this discussion to identify direct and indirect cues coming from students and parents, of the distress they feel about the possible loss of educational services. A discussion of appropriate strategies for dealing with these issues can help teachers maintain their sense of professionalism.

Case Collaboration is a meeting in which a particular case is the focus of discussion. Case collaboration meetings are referred to by other titles as child study team meetings, interdisciplinary team meetings, and planning and placement team meetings. Most of these meetings have the individual case as their focus. The meeting may include a number of specialists such as the psychologist and social worker, speech pathologist, reading consultant, and the teachers currently working, or who will work, with the child in question. The point of the collaboration is to consider the case from a variety of relevant perspectives to increase understanding of the meaning of the behavior in an effort to design the best interventions and programs possible for the child. Classroom interventions attempted are discussed and instructional alternatives which may be helpful are explored in the following Interdisciplinary Team Meeting:

Renee, the occupational therapist, expressed concern about Tommy's unwillingness to stay in his seat during her session with him. The principal pointed out that this behavior was a signal and asked the team members to tune in to what Tommy might be feeling about the session with the occupational therapist. His teacher commented that she noted that children often seemed uncomfortable when called out of the room for a special session. The social worker suggested he might feel "singled out" and embarrassed about having to see the occupational therapist. Maybe he felt it was a stigma. The principal asked the occupational therapist to share some of her conversation with Tommy when he arrived at the session. Perhaps we could put our heads together and come up with a way of addressing the underlying anxiety he may be feeling which may lead to his inability to stay focused on task. We may need to consider how we prepare children like Tommy for special sessions of any kind.

Group Supervision is an extension of individual supervision discussed in the previous chapter. It may be used to supplement supervision work with individual teachers. When the principal believes that other teachers may make a valuable contribution to the development of an individual, group supervision may serve a useful purpose. In the following example, the principal suggests that the discussion which was taking place between herself and a teacher about dealing with disruptive students could be improved if a few of the experienced faculty were involved. The teacher agreed to the suggestion and the principal invited three veteran teachers to a group supervision meeting that went as follows:

The principal began the meeting by explaining that Sandy, a new third grade teacher, was having real difficulty with a few disruptive students who seemed to keep her "on edge" constantly. Sandy explained "I seem to be yelling at them constantly using most of my energy to keep them "in line." The principal then asked each teacher to share their techniques and methods of dealing with these students. At the end of the meeting Sandy said that she felt much better about her situation, realizing that other teachers had similar problems which they learned to overcome. The three veteran teachers offered a support system for Sandy. They agreed to stop in her classroom for short periods of time to offer other suggestions and they invited her to visit their rooms. This type of collaboration strengthens the culture of the faculty and builds its capacity for work.

It is important to note that the same conversation about the same disruptive students can have strikingly different focuses depending upon the purpose of the session. The group purpose determines what is in the foreground of the discussion and what is in the background. As group supervision, this excerpt focused on the teacher and her development of skills for dealing with disruptive students. The teacher was in the foreground and the student example was in the background. In case consultation, the same discussion of disruptive students would have focused on the students rather than the teacher. In a staff meeting, the focus might be on policies of the school in relation to disruptive students. In an in-service meeting (next section), the focus might be on the subject area of disruptive students with the same conversation providing an example to tie theory to practice. It is important to be clear about the purpose of the specific meeting so that the subject in the foreground of the discussion is well understood. Problems can occur, for example, when a teacher shares a problem with a disruptive student for what he/she thinks is case consultation and suddenly begins to experience the discussion as group supervision. Clarity on the purpose of the discussion can increase free expression for the principal and the teachers.

In-service Training meetings focus on the consideration of instructional ideas and techniques by teachers. Ideas are the focus of discussions which share experience and perspectives on the use and function of instructional techniques. The general purposes served by these meetings is to promote professional growth by deepening teachers' understanding of instruction through listening and sharing experiences. Outside resource people are common in such meetings as new ideas are considered and discussed.

Inservice meetings are particularly useful when school districts are introducing new programs such as preschool classes or the use of computers. These meetings may also be used when considering philosophical shifts such as developmental verses basic skills approaches or integration verses categorical special education orientations. The views of staff members from other school districts who have had experiences with these service delivery models can provide crucial insights into the strengths and weaknesses of alternatives being considered for adoption. Inservice meetings provide an appropriate vehicle for these and many other discussions related to program development. The following meeting illustrates a case in point:

Teachers in grade one, a veteran staff, were adamant in their resistance to attempting a whole language approach to reading instruction. Mrs. Matthews, the school principal, scheduled a meeting with the kindergarten and first grade teachers. She encouraged them to express their reservations and she expressed empathy for their feelings and doubts as they discussed the relative merits of the whole language model.

A presentation by a consultant was arranged to review the major elements of the model. A particular emphasis was placed on presenting resource materials for teachers. While the first grade teachers continued to express skepticism, they were willing to try some of the activities which some of the other teachers were implementing. The principal stressed the experimental nature of the project. Additional meetings were scheduled to analyze the effects of their efforts and the model. Encouraging open expression of doubts and objections appeared to quell the teacher's resistance.

Accomplishing Faculty Group Purposes

The principal needs to clarify the general purposes of group meetings with teachers and obtain feedback on their investment in those purposes. When a mutual agreement is formed with teachers on the purpose of a meeting and the role of the principal, a tentative working contract is reached. The principal then begins the task of monitoring the contract and helping teachers to work together to serve group purposes.

This contracting process involves making an opening statement in which the principal spells out his/her sense of the purposes of group sessions. This provides a structure for the group sessions which is essential if the faculty is to develop the freedom to use the meetings constructively. A request for feedback from the faculty on their sense of the use of the meeting completes this element of the contracting process. Contracting, or recontracting, is always possible, even with a group that has met for a long time. The principal may say, for example, "I think it would be useful to talk about these meetings and my role in them. Perhaps we can discuss our views and reach an agreement on both issues."

The following sections in this chapter focus on a number of issues and problems which make it difficult for faculty groups to function together. Teachers will often resist fulfilling the various purposes for meetings.

The reasons for this behavior are frequently related to the group's culture for work which is discussed in the section on the work phase in groups. If administrators are consciously aware of potential obstacles, they may be able to ameliorate their effects through careful planning or by addressing the underlying issues.

The Principal's Role

Because there is often ambiguity and confusion around the principal's role in working with groups of teachers, clarifying this role early in the process helps to avoid difficulty. It should be noted that efforts to clarify the role of the principal are usually tested and, if results are positive, teachers will develop confidence in the agreed upon contract. If the principal promises that criticism will be accepted, teachers will likely test her/him to determine reactions before total candor is expressed. If negative feedback is encountered, teachers may withdraw and the principal may lose a valuable opportunity to develop a constructive relationship with them. The true leadership style of the principal will emerge over time within the daily routine operation of the school.

Generic leadership styles have been represented in the literature over the past thirty or more years. Common terms used to describe such styles include laissez-faire, autocratic, and democratic with respective behaviors generally accepted within each of these styles. Previous experiences of teachers may include authoritarian principals who attempted to dominate the school using their authority; laissez-faire leaders who pretended to have no authority while using other means to get their way; and democratic leaders who attempted to develop their authority from within the group. These terms represent model forms of leadership behavior that are commonly understood in our society.

The autocratic principal who may take responsibility for the group, may police teachers into apparently submissive participants who demonstrate their feelings through passive resistance or agreeing to decisions while not really committing to them. The illusion of work is often the result of this form of leadership. Although this type of leadership may offer structural control, little freedom for group actualization and ownership may be common complications. Teachers may take little or no responsibility for making such groups work well and they may feel that the principal "runs the show."

In contrast, the laissez-faire approach appears to offer no responsibility directly to the leader. The principal may ask teachers "what are your concerns today?" This approach appears to offer freedom, but the absence of structure may ultimately be as restrictive as the authoritarian approach. For example, discussions may ramble onto topics having little or no relevance to the issues at hand, but the lack of structure permits them to continue. The effect may be to allow attention and interest to wane with a subsequent decline in willingness to participate rendering the group ineffective. A demand for work may effectively redirect such discussions into productive channels.

In some situations the principal, knowing that teachers are not able to work together effectively, may take the opportunity to make it appear that control must be exercised to get necessary things done. The effect may be that the laissez-faire strategy overtly appears to offer freedom when, in reality, the supervisor or principal exercises significant control over teachers though more subtle measures. The principal may recognize that inactivity and lack of decisiveness may force the group to relinquish control to the leader. The effect of faculty group structure which is too loose may be that all of the really important decisions affecting the school will be made away from their group. The faculty in such situations may demand that the leader act more autocratically, creating another set of problems entirely. Dreary faculty meetings, passive aggression, and group depression may ultimately result.

The laissez-faire approach in some schools attempts to give each teacher a fair voice in the decisions of the school. If the current movement to empower teachers results in eliminating autocratic leadership that precipitated it but it allows an incorrect understanding of group leadership to serve as the foundation of a form of colleagueship, it may ultimately be dysfunctional to the overall operation of the school. This may be one of the potential dangers of the current movement to empower teachers. When decisiveness is required, as it eventually is in most group situations, leaderless forms of group operation often become incapable of acting to solve group dilemmas.

The qualities of democratic leadership may be most closely related to the functioning principal-faculty leadership role suggested in this book, but the element of external authority is not included. The internal appointment of a group leader, a primary element of democratic leadership, relies entirely upon the group for authority. When, or if, the group no longer supports the leader, effectiveness wanes. Reliance entirely upon internal sources of authority is a weakness of the democratic form of leadership.

Democratic leadership may offer the most appropriate means of involving teachers in the determination and implementation of directions taken by the school. It may also offer the best opportunity for a sense of group achievement, enhanced teacher morale, and ultimately get many important tasks of the school completed. Other forms of leadership may permit short-term solutions which provide a "quick fix," but they are likely to be dysfunctional in the long term.

A significant difficulty of democratic leadership is that the principal's formal authority is derived from the school board, not from teachers. The principal is an external leader appointed by a legitimate source of external authority representing the citizens of the local school district. She/he is responsible to that authority for the operation of the school. Principals may use this external authority to help or hinder their effectiveness with their teachers. Clearly, the authority of the principal is externally derived. However, the ability of the principal to lead a group of teachers is internally derived.

It is not uncommon for faculty groups to attempt to create a more democratic atmosphere by having the chair of the meeting rotate among teachers. While this can be a useful structure under certain circumstances, it does not change the basic dynamics of the group. The principal still maintains the external authority of the role. When crucial issues are raised, one can see the faculty turning to the principal even though she/he is not officially in the chair.

If teachers understand and acknowledge the difference in these notions about internal leadership and external authority, it may serve to clarify important boundaries in the principal's role, reducing or avoiding ambiguity and conflict. The relationship between teachers and the principal on various decisions needs to be articulated. On some issues, the principal may be responsible only for helping teachers to arrive at decisions which concern them. Other issues may involve teacher input into the process with the principal making the final decision. Decisions which rely upon mutual agreement may also be appropriate in some situations. When teachers are aware of the degree of their involvement in specific school decisions in which they are expected to participate, they may be more likely to support and implement them as well. Achieving such an understanding with teachers permits the principal to represent both the interests of the board and the staff, maintaining honest, open communications in the supervisory relationship. Other styles of leadership may permit decisions to be made more quickly, but they may also be less effective in the ways that teachers support them or not support them.

The Work Phase in Groups

Three issues that are central to working effectively with teacher groups are: developing a positive group work culture, handling individual/group concerns, and managing conflict in the group. Developing a positive work culture enables the supervisor and the teachers to construct and implement solutions effectively for the myriad of issues that confront them during the school year. Dealing with individual/group issues with teachers and handling conflict in the group are common issues which the principal must resolve and they are discussed in succeeding sections. Contracting, establishing the relationship between the principal and the faculty group which can be included in the beginning phase or the work phase, is the focus of the next section dealing with developing a culture for work.

Supervision work with teachers is conducted by the principal in both formal and informal settings. Alternative forms of formal teacher groups were described previously with respect to group purpose: staff meetings, case collaboration, group supervision, and inservice training. Informal interactions in groupings composed of teachers, support staff, children, and parents may also be powerful forces in schools. These informal interactions may be a positive or negative influence on established school purposes. They occur as part of the daily operation of school buildings. The examples in the following section involve both formal and informal groupings of teachers. They are intended to show similarities in the dynamics and the functional role of the principal using interactive skills in each setting.

Developing an Effective Faculty Culture

When a group of teachers who work together in the same building comes together something is created which is more than the mere sum of its parts. This "organism" can be called the group-as-a-whole. This group has its own set of properties which are not directly observable. What can be observed is group and individual behaviors which result from these properties. The properties of this faculty group include norms or standards of behavior which become group expectations. In some cases, behavior may be inferred from inaction by members of the group. Informal group norms and taboos may be inferred from their effect of constraining the behavior of teacher members as well.

For example, our society has a definite taboo against the open expression of anger. Suppression or preference for the indirect expression of anger in accordance with generally acceptable rules is a common norm in our society. When teachers enter their work group, they bring a tradition or convention of social prohibition which forbids the direct or open discussion of anger. When the teachers in a faculty group share this prohibition, a group norm is formed which affects member behavior. Groups enforce norms by the use of sanctions, which act as a form of punishment when norms are violated. Sanctions may involve giving the silent treatment in the teachers' lounge to a member who violated a group norm in a meeting. The power of these group norms is well documented (Joyce, Hersh, and Mckibbin, 1983, 68) and significant as the need for group acceptance is felt by all teachers to some extent.

The norms of a faculty culture are not formally codified or written but they are well understood by the teachers in the group. Difficulties may be posed by the norms of the faculty work group. For example, if the culture of the group incorporates norms against "rate-busting"—volunteering to do extra work or go beyond the contract, and a teacher volunteers, group sanctions may be directed against her/him. In another example, the silent treatment is one such sanction used by teachers when the supervisor violates the norm of nonintrusion in their classrooms (Joyce, 1983). In any close working relationship, occasional friction that generates anger must be expected. If the teacher group has norms which forbid the open expression of anger, the principal may never understand why teachers are irate. It is especially important to note that norms which suppress the open expression of anger may also function to suppress the expression of caring by group members as well. Suppressed feelings of anger by members may lie dormant under the surface and become obstacles to the operation of the group as they surface in other forms of behavior, which may include individual apathy and teacher burnout. The following sections focus on norms or rules governing appropriate behavior.

A positive function of the work group culture is to provide teachers with some degree of certainty about behavior. Group norms may be supportive, such as rallying to a colleague in some difficulty, or they may be negative, such as giving a teacher who violates a norm against open criticism of a colleague the "cold shoulder" in the teacher's lounge. The norms which, to some degree, govern teacher behavior may also be obstacles to productive cooperation with the principal. Norms which inhibit collaborative relationships with supervisors prevent an effective work culture from developing within a faculty.

Teacher groups may be expected to reflect general societal norms and others which are more unique and specialized. Problems with group norms, which become obstacles inhibiting productive relationships, are almost inevitable between the principal and a faculty. The role of the principal or school supervisor in such cases is to identify the obstacles, bring them to the attention of the faculty, and work with them to develop new norms or rules which are functionally related to productive work. This process is what is meant by developing a positive work culture. Norms which restrict open, honest communication between the principal and the teachers or among teachers are such obstacles.

The principal's task is to monitor both the content agenda and the process of group work with the faculty and call attention to the need for adjustments and modifications as they become necessary. In this way the principal may develop a teacher group culture which is productive and which functions to solve school problems through the involvement of the entire faculty.

One response to this suggestion by practicing principals may be that time does not permit them to function in this way. It may be argued, in response, that difficulties created by a dysfunctional work group may be the cause of many of the problems which consume a great deal of time. Instead of overlooking disgruntled and hostile faces in a faculty meeting, the principal may try to address their feelings directly and then commit to a mutually workable relationship with them. In this way faculty meetings may actually be something teachers look forward to instead of dreading. Once a supervisor overcomes the fear associated with opening issues, which have never been discussed with the faculty, the actual process itself may be less threatening. In many cases where no real effort to unlock such problems has been made for some time, a degree of comfort with the status quo may exist where both the principal and the teachers fear change. This has been referred to as the illusion of work and it offers some degree of safety and predictability to all parties because it insures that no real change is expected.

The Boring Faculty Meeting

One of the most common complaints from teachers is that faculty meetings are boring. Principals often complain that teachers just sit there, impervious to everything, hoping the clock will strike the magic moment of the end of the meeting. When union contracts specify the duration of faculty meetings, teachers may stand up and leave without regard to the comments of the principal. Recognizing that teachers are bored and facing a time limit, principals may put their heads down and plow through the agenda with or without the attention of the faculty.

Apparently, boring faculty meetings may in fact contain topics which are so relevant that the staff is reluctant to pursue the discussion. At other times the topics may be perceived as irrelevant by them. It is important for principals to examine the implications of what appears on the surface to be boredom. Revealing underlying feelings may help staff members to confront important issues which cause great anxiety. The principal may encounter both resistance and reluctance by staff members to share hidden feelings. The skills suggested in previous chapters are useful to the principal in helping teachers to share difficult feelings, thus freeing them to focus on other issues. The following meeting is an example:

Mr. Cento, middle school principal, presented the third bus duty schedule in a two-week period at the faculty meeting. Dick Cable, a physical education teacher, expressed concern that some teachers were assigned regularly and others were given exemption from duty. Bob Heins, a science teacher, and ever the diplomat, said the topic had been discussed to exhaustion and suggested that the group move on to the next item on the agenda in the interest of time. When Mr. Cento went on with the agenda, he began to notice side conversations among staff while other faculty appeared to be staring out the window or looking as though they had other things on their minds.

Suspicious that the bus duty issue was still festering, Mr. Cento decided to broach the subject again and said, "I'm wondering if everyone is finally comfortable with the bus duty situation?" Dick Cable snickered at the question as he spoke out, "Special education teachers always get away with less work than the rest of us. They have smaller classes than the rest of us and now they have no bus duty at all."

Reluctant to encourage dissension, but sensing that discussion was necessary, Mr. Cento suggested that they discuss Dick's concern. Brenda

Mattison, a special education teacher, countered, saying, "We teach with the most difficult children in this school and many of them are not wanted in regular classes, even in gym."

Sensing that real discussion was about to erupt in the midst of confrontation, Mr. Cento decided to encourage the conflict. He was careful to intervene when the discussion became too hostile but, generally, he just encouraged both sides to listen to each other.

Eventually, the opponents were able to cite the underlying perceptions which framed their current feelings. Mr. Cento reminded the group that each faculty member had job responsibilities which were challenging, though different. As he did, he pointed out that all staff were experiencing stress at this time and that it may have made it hard for them to understand the stress of their colleagues. He asked the group to think about ways in which the bus duty schedule could be revised to be more acceptable to everyone. He also suggested that they take time to think about how they and he might be helpful to each other around the issue of stress in general.

In this case, the principal realized that the group was apparently evading work when staff members began to show disinterest in the agenda. He was suspicious that bus duty was a taboo subject because of the feelings it may evoke in the staff, but he elected to pursue the discussion. He challenged the group and they voiced their real concerns. If the principal had been reluctant to invite this discussion, the issue may have remained under the surface, and it may have become a significant obstacle to productive work among the faculty.

Individual Roles within the Group Context

Although the norms which characterize the culture of a particular teacher work group affect the functioning of the group, personality factors and individual qualities of members also play a significant part in the operation of the group. The notion of role illustrates the transformation of the personality of the individual teacher within the context of group operation. Images which often surface within faculty groups may be characterized by the roles of defiant member, informal leader, and withdrawn member. These roles are explored in the following sections.

It is helpful to note that the particular group context is important to understanding the suggested roles of individual teachers. The behavior suggested in the following roles is, in part, a function of the social relationships of the respective individual teachers as members of the faculty group. The staff group must be viewed as a dynamic system in which the behavior of any member is, in part, affected by the interaction in the group. A common mistake is to attribute particular behaviors as solely a result of a teacher's personality.

The Defiant Member. Known to be an outspoken critic of the administration, the defiant or resistant faculty group member may take the position that "they tried this five years ago and it didn't work then so it's a waste of our valuable time now." Joyce and McKibbin (1982, 37) describe resistant behavior as viewing any change with suspicion, openly and surreptitiously opposing development. They suggest that the informal faculty group is significantly controlled and stifled by such members.

Principals often indicate that the elimination of one such member from their faculty would have a significant renewal effect. In reality, the absence of one such member is likely create another teacher ready to assume the role. A common reaction to the defiant teacher by the principal is to become defensive or aggressive, or both. In the following example, the principal reacted defensively, attempting to use the group to cutoff the defiant member:

"I explained the effect of the budget reductions by the Board at the meeting last night. I then asked the faculty if they had any suggestions for areas where we could find the money with less harm to the children. During my explanation Peter sat with an angry smirk on his face. I knew he was likely to gripe about the situation, so I avoided eye contact with him.

Two questions were asked about the cutback and one suggestion was made. I credited the group with a good start when Peter spoke out, "This is just an exercise in futility." I was upset that he cut the productive discussion off just as it began and allowed the meeting to turn into a gripe session. I retorted with: "I'm sorry that you feel that we are wasting our time Peter. Your attitude is not constructive and I'm sure others here agree with me." During the rest of the meeting the faculty was lethargic and not really committed to the discussion. Peter stared quietly out the window for most of the remainder of the meeting.

The principal's response to Peter's quip effectively cut off the faculty discussion, preventing them from expressing their real feelings on the budget reduction issue. They would quickly return to their condemnations in the teachers' lounge the next day where the principal was not part of the discussion. If the principal really wants honest communication, the defiant member may be considered an ally as a spokesperson for the feelings of the faculty. In the following situation, instead of cutting off objections, the principal attempts to encourage discussion into the meaning behind the outburst:

"During our last meeting I felt that Peter's comment was not useful and I cut him off. I never realized how uncomfortable I was discussing the cutback. I want to apologize. I think we need to bring the issue out in the open again for discussion so we all can express our thinking on the issue. Do you agree with me?"

Tom said that every year we seem to be in the same place with cuts expected from budgets which are already slim. Bob said that we are being penalized for doing an excellent job of asking for only what we needed in the original budget. Other schools in the district seem to ask for more than they need and then they are able to reduce the budget with no pain.

I confided in the group that I was beginning to wonder where this discussion was going and what my role would be. Val suggested that a real case could be made for our building on a comparative basis and that I should take it to the superintendent. I suggested that we do the analysis together and invite the superintendent to our school for a group meeting. They became animated and issues were raised about conditions in other buildings that they knew of that would help our cause. Clearly, they wanted the opportunity to try to protect our school from further budget cuts.

The second meeting served to encourage teachers to express their feelings and formulate a strategy that may solve their problem. If the attempt to convince the superintendent is unsuccessful, the staff will return to the task of reduction in a better frame of mind than before. If they are successful, a great deal of positive morale will be generated. In any case, the principal has improved the working relationship with the teachers by treating negative reactions positively.

Another example of the defiant role as an ally is the teacher who begins to arrive late on a frequent basis, and/or generally stares out the window during the entire faculty meeting. The principal's initial reaction to Joe's fourth late walk-in was anger and raised eyebrows. After this first reaction the principal reached behind the symptom in an effort to determine the source of the behavior:

"The meeting had begun and we were on the second item on the agenda when Joe walked into the room. He had been late for the past three meetings and the staff began to expect him to walk in late. I stopped as he sat down and asked if he would share the feelings behind his apparent disinterest in the meetings. He glared at me, then said that these meetings were a total waste of his time. With papers to correct and lessons to prepare, attending faculty meetings, which never seemed to deal with the real issues, was unbearable. I responded that I, too, had other things to do but I had to attend faculty meetings because I was the principal. As the faculty laughed, I asked if others agreed with Joe and if they felt we should revise our meetings and improve interest in the discussions."

The remainder of the faculty meeting revolved around the need to revise the agenda for our meetings. They were agreed that all items of general communication should be circulated in a weekly memo, and only matters which required discussion should be on the agenda. They also expressed the feeling that superficial discussion was a waste of their time and only decisions which required their genuine participation should be included. Joe, who was active in this discussion, revealed that there were a number of important issues in the building that needed to be discussed such as students skipping sixth period without being caught, and the use of the lavatories for smoking. As often may be the case, the teacher who appears to be resistant may be performing a role for the group by voicing concern for important issues which are just beneath the surface of the discussion. Behavior that may have been interpreted as the desire to eliminate faculty meetings was, in reality, a concern for making them more substantive and purposeful.

The situations just described were examples of the defiant teacher playing a functional role for the faculty as a group. It is also possible in a larger school for a subgroup of a faculty, such as the coaches or the math department, to play the defiant role for the larger group.

The Informal Group Leader. The principal is the formal or external leader of the teaching faculty because the source of her/his authority of position is the Board of Education. The informal or internal leader (or leaders) of the faculty emerge from internal processes to help the group solve problems. One informal group leader was the former president of the Teachers' Union during a bitter strike. She was looked to for leadership by the staff whenever they faced a difficult situation. When the faculty becomes directly opposed to the administration, as with a grievance, the informal leader may also be thought of by the principal as the defiant member.

Principals, feeling insecure in their roles, may view the informal leader as a challenge to their authority. This is particularly true when informal leaders hold influential positions in the teachers' union and call regular meetings of the staff to discuss the administration of the employment contract in the building. These meetings are often called after faculty meetings, and since only teachers may attend, concern by the principal is natural. However, the situation may also be viewed conversely with the defiant-informal group leader being thought of as an ally by the principal, as presented in the previous examples. From this perspective, the principal would regard the informal leader as a natural and functionally necessary part of the group process and a source of valuable information about teacher feelings and concerns, which may be useful in work toward solutions to problems in the school.

The Withdrawn Group Member. Principals often are concerned about teachers who appear attentive but seldom contribute or participate in faculty meetings. Overt techniques, such as asking direct questions in the meeting to such teachers, often result in them politely declining to respond. When these efforts are repeated, the situation may result in further withdrawal or antipathy. It is important to recognize that the withdrawn teacher may be a reluctant participant in many areas of life and thus prefers to behave accordingly in faculty meetings. One strategy that may offer involvement without pressure is for the principal to speak to the teacher outside of the group and to inquire about the participation. It would be crucial to reassure the teacher that the principal realizes teachers can be actively involved without speaking. The conversation is not meant to pressure the teacher. Rather, the approach is to offer help for the teacher to get involved, if she/he wishes. This may involve a special sign given by the withdrawn teacher to the principal indicating an interest in participating in the discussion.

Teachers who monopolize discussion at faculty meetings may also become obstacles to group participation. Such individuals may annoy other teachers but they will seldom be objected to openly during faculty meetings. The principal may ask these participants if they occasionally feel that they are being used by the group because they seem to "carry the ball" for the rest of the faculty. The principal may remind the group that although some may speak more than others, they all must take responsibility and contribute to the group process in some way. This approach may broaden participation without disparaging those who speak too frequently.

The role of the principal as mediator in the examples just given was to find the connection between the individual teacher and the group. From this perspective the principal may be able to suggest common objectives which may have been hidden in unexpressed feelings of the group. Identifying with the individual to the exclusion of the group, or vice/versa, may result in the principal being cutoff from helping with the dynamic interaction of the two forces. Integration of the mediating function enables the principal to identify with the individual and the group at the same time.

Mediating Teacher Group Conflict

Principals often find that formal or informal conflicts among faculty members are very difficult to resolve. A typical scenario may involve a teacher reporting to the principal that another teacher never watches her children in the cafeteria: "She just sits there, oblivious to her students yelling and acting-out etc." The situation may become more difficult when the principal suggests that the teacher approach the colleague in question with the problem and hears a response like: "That's what you get paid for, you're the principal." A common response in these situations is for the principal to agree to talk to the offender with the proviso that, "Please don't say that I told you this?" It is understandable that such requests are made and, in many cases unfortunate that they are accepted because they often lead to hard feelings and no solution. In a typical follow-up discussion by the principal, the teacher responds with a defensive retort, saying that her students are no worse than those of Mrs. ———. This kind of push/pull contest is often a no win situation which leaves hard feelings for some time after the incident.

The role of mediator suggests that the principal, by cultivating a positive work culture, may help teachers to accept responsibility for solving their own conflicts. This may also enable the principal to manage her/his role more easily. The primary task of the principal in such matters is that of facilitator, helping teachers to help themselves, rather than as the problem solver. This means that the principal will rarely accept the responsibility for problem solving except in situations where continuity of service and strong opposition require it.

When teachers know that the supervisor will not automatically accept responsibility as arbitrator, and/or judge, fewer problems end up in the principal's office. A significant amount of the principal's time and energy could easily be taken with such matters if the role were not otherwise clearly defined. In addition, teachers who work together must be responsible for their professional and social relationships. The principal is not responsible for developing or managing patterns of friendships among teachers. Productive instructional relationships among teachers are expected and required regardless of social relationships.

When informal conflict among teachers affects the quality of instruction provided to children, it becomes crucial that the principal become involved. The goal of involvement in these matters is to develop the capacity of the faculty culture for self-correction. This may be accomplished by helping teachers to develop the ability to solve their own problems. It may also reduce the number of such problems brought to the principal. The general approach in dealing with these problems is for the principal to avoid magnifying the content of the dilemma and to focus on the process by meeting with the teachers involved, "face to face," and helping them to work out a solution themselves. The following example illustrates the role of the principal in group conflict:

During the weeks before school began, negotiations between the Board and the Teachers' Association broke down with no movement on either side. The week before school was to begin, the teachers voted to strike. Although the vote was close, they agreed to walk the picketline, showing parents that they were united. One elementary school in the district was opening a new addition that year with eleven new teachers joining the staff. On the first day of school, the new teachers drove into the parking lot and walked through the sparse picketers into the school. The busses were turned back by the administration district-wide and there was no school that day. On the second day of the strike parents, substitutes, and the same group of teachers came to work across the picket line. The strike ended that day with all teachers returning to work on the third day of school. By the second week of school the battle lines were drawn between those who picketed and those who did not. Bitterness and resentment marked the relations between the two factions. At first, the principal tried to ignore the tension in the hope it would go away by itself. The principal decided to step in when it did not dissipate and bring the factions together. The meeting began with the principal's comments:

"I thought we should talk about the first week of school. It has been hard for us to work together and I sense the stress building with each day of school. If we can get this out in the open and talk about it, it may be easier for us to work together. If we leave the situation as it is, it will be a very difficult school year for all of us and the children. My role is to help you talk to each other constructively and listen to each other carefully. Now, who wants to start?"

After a long pause, which the principal "rode out" by waiting, the discussion began with Mike, a veteran of ten years in the building, complaining that all the effort to reach a fair settlement was for naught with these teachers crossing the line. It became clear that deep feelings of enmity were held on both sides. Issues of family and tenure were raised by the new teachers. The discussion went on well beyond the four o'clock closing time for faculty meetings. The meeting concluded with both sides asking for another time to discuss the issues, soon. The principal agreed to set up another meeting the following week.

It would be important at the follow-up meeting, that the principal focus the discussion on the issue of the impact of the tension on the operation of the school. For example, after the venting of staff feelings, the principal could ask: "In what ways do you see this stress our ability to work effectively together? We may not be able to resolve the anger here, but we do have a responsibility to work together professionally."

This example illustrates the need to focus on the process, not the content of faculty conflicts. It would have been impossible to manage the arguments on both sides. Holding both sides responsible for some form of beginning resolution in a face to face meeting presented the opportunity to vent the powerful feelings that were hidden just below the surface of interaction among the faculty members. The difficulty in this situation would not disappear, but the actions taken by the principal would begin to heal the wounds and reduce the bitterness.

Teacher Group/District Conflicts

The dilemma of being caught in the middle is one the most common and troublesome confronting the building principal. As a member of the superintendent's staff, the principal feels a sense of loyalty to the central office. At the same time, the daily operation of the building and work with the faculty develop a deep identification with the feelings of teachers. New policies, procedures, and requirements often "handed down" to teachers from the central office may not be easily integrated into daily classroom work with children. The causes of the conflict between classroom teachers and the district administration may vary in schools, but the position of the principal is the same. If the principal identifies with the central office position on a policy, she/he may risk being viewed as a betrayer by the faculty, and the opposite position may result in an accusation by the superintendent of not being a team player. One response to this dilemma is a "blame it on the top" mentality, suggesting that such circumstances are inevitably resolved in favor of the hierarchy of authority, so why bother to disagree? The "you can't fight city hall syndrome," may be one of the reasons supporting the conclusion that teachers feel powerless with respect to change at any other than the classroom level (Joyce et al., 1982).

The role of the principal as mediator suggests that choosing sides in such conflicts may not be productive or necessary. Rather, the principal should invest in the need for, and the value of, process in dealing with such dilemmas. This position is useful in helping teachers to express negative feelings instead of allowing them to grow beneath the surface and appear as indirect expressions in other forms, which may affect the provision of services to children.

The suggested role of the principal is not one of absolute neutrality on all issues. Rather, it calls for honest expression of the principal's own view and clear delineation of the part he/she will play in the process of problem solving. This means the role of the principal is not dictated by personal opinion of the content of disputes but, rather by the process of finding productive alternatives which serve as the objective for his/her involvement with the parties. Demanding that both parties treat the issues in the conflict honestly means that the principal's personal view is not pivotal in the quest for solutions. He/she will communicate staff feelings and views to the central office, whether she/he agrees with the position of the staff or with the central office. The reverse is also true.

The mediation role of the principal is not an exercise in conflict avoidance but, rather, a quest to confront conflict openly and honestly. It calls for bringing issues which may have been churning just below the surface with faculty members into the open. Such issues are often discussed in the teacher's lounge or in the corridors, but they are seldom openly discussed with the principal. Confronting these hidden agenda issues with real communication may occasionally require the principal to take a position as advocate for the faculty in confronting the administration. Occasionally, the course of these disputes, particularly those that end up in the grievance procedure, may find both teachers and the administration losing sight of their common goals regarding children. However, the principal must remain committed to finding common means of accomplishing objectives shared by the teachers and the administration in providing instruction to children. The mediation role of the principal calls for providing an open process of problem-solving based on honest communication which preserves the dignity of both parties. The process focuses on the need to explore alternatives which facilitate the accomplishment of mutual interests of both the teachers and the administration in the provision of instructional services to children. In this way the principal also serves as a primary advocate for the children of the school district. Haller and Strike (1986, 88) refer to this as promoting a "fair fight" in which the administrator helps each party to recognize the legitimate rights of the other.

Fundamental to the success in the role of mediator is the principal's view of change. If a positive regard for change in the school is reflected in the principal's behavior, teachers are more likely to strive to improve school conditions. Principals may also bring an apathetic attitude reflecting a view that schools are immutable. This may be a reflection of their own feeling of incapability to influence the system. If the school district culture has discouraged efforts to grow, administrators may fear being accused of not being "team players." In addition, principals are extremely busy with matters involved in running the schools. Discipline problems, parent concerns, areas of the building that need attention at certain times of the day, and a host of other time-consuming issues may deter them from the task of initiating change. Fear of potential effects, lack of time, and a sense of futility may all constrain principals from change efforts.

Similarly, when the integration of teachers into a static school culture saps individual initiative, a general discouragement with the prospect of change may dispose many individuals and the group negatively on many worthwhile change initiatives. The principal may help teachers to understand and deal with these beliefs by explaining the simultaneous openness and resistance involved in the dynamics of change in schools. This may help teachers to realize that the lack of immediate success of an effort to change the system does not mean complete failure, and that resistance from the system and other members of the group is a normal and expected part of the growth process.

The Principal Caught in the Middle

The following example illustrates the principal in the middle between the central office and the teachers. The situation stems from the election of several new members to the school board with a common interest in reform and the "back to basics" mentality. Soon after the organizational meeting of the board, a new mandatory homework policy was adopted. It was rumored to have been a copy of a neighboring school district policy. The new policy dictated required hours of homework by grade and subject to be assigned. Teachers were to correct, grade, and return all homework within one day of completion. Anticipating resistance to the policy, the board offered no period of consideration but insisted that it be put into effect one week from the date of the meeting. Copies of the policy were sent to the teachers the next day. The teachers were incensed by the policy, and the faculty room at Shattuck Elementary School buzzed with angry fervor.

After discussions with the faculty, the principal decided to talk to the superintendent to explain how the teachers felt in her building. The purpose of this meeting was for the building principal to accurately communicate the teachers' thoughts and feelings in a way which reduces defensive and aggressive reactions from the superintendent. The objective of the meeting was to identify and strengthen areas of common concern between the teaching staff and the central office. Note the use of the supervisory skills discussed in the early chapters. The meeting went as follows:

"I told the superintendent that I wanted to explore ways that we may be able to deal with the faculty reactions to the homework policy. I stated that I was not sure that anything would help, but making the effort was important to all concerned. I asked if he could give me some reactions to the thinking I had done on the problem so far.

The superintendent indicated that he would be happy to discuss the issue but since this board had a "mind of it's own" he was not sure that anything could be achieved by the effort. He went on to describe the cautions which he pointed out to the board about adverse reactions and the need for involvement of the teachers before such actions were taken, regardless of how well intended they may be. The board reacted aggressively to this and told him that he had to support them or they would find a superintendent who would. He indicated that he knew then that they had no regard for his warning and he was powerless to stop them.

As I listened, I gained some insights into the problems which the superintendent faced when he tried to protect the interests of the teaching staff with the board. I shared those with him and then returned to the present problem by indicating that it may help if the teachers knew that he had attempted to protect their interests and that direct feedback from teachers might be very helpful to him in dealing with the board. If nothing else came from such a meeting, at least the teachers would feel that they were given a chance to speak out on the issue. I further said that the faculty would appreciate knowing that he did speak out for them and that this may be a positive step in dealing with the actual implementation of the homework policy.

The superintendent said that he was not sure that such a meeting would help the situation because he was not sure how candid he could be. The board felt that many teachers were not giving homework because of the extra work involved, and he did not want to alienate them with this information. He also said that he could not afford to be viewed as disloyal to the board. I told him that I could appreciate his position and that I was in a similar position between him and my faculty. I further indicated that in such circumstances I had tried to be honest with the teachers and they seemed to understand that I had to deal with the issues from both the administrative and instructional perspectives, trying to be as helpful to the actual teaching situation as possible. I then said that my discussion with him was an example of what I was suggesting.

I then asked the superintendent if he was concerned about the meeting and the possibility of outright hostility leading to a hardening of positions. The teachers were angry and I wouldn't blame him if he were worried about facing them. He said that the thing he feared most was utter silence and then he thought that they would just sit there and stare at him with passive hostility. I told him that the teachers would be more likely to share their feelings if he assured them that he understood how they feel and that they were free to say what they felt openly, and he would do the same. He agreed to the meeting and I said that I was grateful for his time."

Mediating the Faculty-Superintendent Conflict

The role of the principal in these situations is to help both the superintendent and the teachers talk and listen to each other. This may call for interventions which keep the discussion honest, convey real feelings, and/or focus on common purposes in working with children. Fear may be an overwhelming obstacle for many teachers, especially when such meetings only occur at times of great stress. It is important for the principal to clarify her/his role in these meetings so that her comments would be more readily understood by both parties. The principal tuned in to the likely silence that may occur and planned to comment, "I know that it's difficult to start, especially with the depth of feeling on the homework issue." She also thought of a simple contracting statement to begin the meeting so that everyone began with the same sense of purpose. "The purpose of this meeting is to discuss both the new homework policy and the way in which the policy was initiated. Since we know there are very strong feeling on these issues, I thought it appropriate for me to concentrate on helping everyone talk and listen to each other. Is this acceptable to all of you?" The principal also recognized that indirect expression of anger and fear, such as sarcasm and passive aggression, were likely in this meeting and that she may have to reach for the honest feelings behind these. The following is a summary of the meeting with the superintendent:

"On the day of the meeting several teachers commented jokingly that they hoped I was ready for the 'shootout.' I responded that I hoped it went well for everyone. Later on, when the meeting began, I made my opening statement. After a moment of silence the teachers began to let their feelings out, slowly at first, then all at once. The superintendent sat there tense and listened carefully to the teachers' comments. Many of the comments were expected because I had shared them in my previous meeting with the superintendent.

After a brief outpouring of comments by the faculty, I said that maybe we should take one issue at a time. I then asked the superintendent where he wanted to start? He began by explaining the board's thinking behind the policy and why it was necessary for everyone to give homework to children. As the superintendent explained the points in the policy, teachers countered with their views, which were quite dissonant from his. It began to look like we were talking in circles, getting nowhere in the discussion.

I interrupted when I saw the discussion going nowhere and I shared that with both sides. Then I explained that other concerns may exist that had not been raised. For example, the teachers had said that this was just another example of lack of concern for them in policy making by the central office and the school board but this had not been said, as yet, to the superintendent. Then I told the teachers that the superintendent had tried to defend them at the meeting by telling the board that such policies should have teacher input before they are adopted. Peter, a fifth grade teacher, asked if it was true that he had tried to involve teachers in the process?

The superintendent shared some of the process which went into the decision on the homework policy. He was very clear that the goals of the homework policy were excellent, but the process of adoption was not appropriate since teachers were not given the opportunity to discuss it with the board. He explained that political pressures on new board members who ran on a back-to-basics campaign spurred them into action with little deliberation. The teachers were listening intently, obviously interested in the superintendent's candid remarks about the process.

Some of the teachers responded with comments letting the superintendent know how upset they were with the fact that a policy, which had so deeply affected them, was enacted with no concern for their work in classrooms with children. The teachers stated that they felt that nobody cared about them. The superintendent then said that it would help him if they could describe the specific problems they found with the policy and suggest ways that the intent of the policy could be accomplished while avoiding the difficulties. I remained silent as the superintendent and the teachers began to work out some modifications and compromises which he would share with the board. He asked if several of the teachers would attend the next meeting if the board agreed to the proposal, to help him explain why these were important to the instructional program."

This meeting did not solve the problems caused by the homework policy, but a positive step was taken toward that end. In addition, the teachers and the superintendent found that they could have a dialogue which, though heated, was constructive. The board accepted the revisions suggested. The teachers were still not happy that a required procedure existed where they once had complete freedom, but a start had been made toward more open communication between the teachers and the board. The skill and courage of the principal must be credited in this vignette, for without the belief that change was possible, the teachers would have felt victimized and morale may have declined further.

Faculty-Principal Relationships

The preceding examples and discussion focused on teacher group interactions in which the principal was the mediator between two forces. In the following paragraphs the sensitive relationship between the principal and the faculty group will be addressed. Common myths that may affect the relationship are that good principals always have positive relationships and only ineffective principals have problems with their teaching staff. The skillful principal deals with problems openly and honestly, including the inevitable mistakes that everyone makes from time to time, instead of pretending that they do not exist. Bringing problems out in the open for discussion and action is part of the foundation of an effective principal-faculty relationship. Some of the issues which affect the relationship are: (1) power and control; (2) the principal as a outsider and; (3) the principal as a source of support and demand.

Power and Control

A central question which teachers often ask when working in groups is who benefits from the meeting? When teachers believe that the group is controlled by the principal and used as a means of achieving his/her own ends. Teachers may feel that they are being used as an instrument by the principal for his/her own benefit. Since the principal is in control of the selection of agenda items, the nature of faculty discussion sessions, and the conclusions from these discussions, teacher participation is often reactive. Great care must be exercised to insure that teachers take responsibility for the effectiveness of the group at meetings. Sessional contracting and other skills have been offered in previous chapters, which help to accomplish this end.

Issues related to the authority of the principal will emerge in different ways at different times in the life of the faculty group. There are unique dynamics in the beginning phase, as discussed in the sections dealing with the new principal. These issues are never fully resolved, reemerging at critical moments during the life of the group. They take on new forms in the ending stage when the principal leaves the job. In the following sections, some of the elements of this authority theme are explored.

The Principal as an Outsider

The principal will always be an "outsider." Even with long experience as a teacher, once the transition is made to administrator, the status of being part of a group changes. For the new principal, this may be one of the more difficult elements of the transition. It is important for the principal to develop a source of support to deal with the isolation imposed by her/his authority.

In a previous example Maureen, a newly appointed elementary principal and former teacher in the building, illustrated the dilemmas faced by the principal as an outsider. The principal is no longer a teacher and subtler clues are found in the reactions of the faculty to various situations. By demonstrating a capacity for empathy, the principal can help to ameliorate the outsider feelings that often accompany the job.

The Principal as a Source of Support and Demand

Despite the fact that the principal is an outsider, the faculty wants and needs her/him to support them. The ability of the principal to convey empathy is an important variable in the relationship with teachers. In addition to the need for support, teachers also need to be pushed into expressing themselves when it may be easier to remain silent and uninvolved. Forcing discussion of issues which are under the surface and strongly felt by teachers by demanding honest expression in group meetings is equally important to a functional supervision relationship. This means insisting that teachers take responsibility for, and participate actively in, group processes. This pushing and insisting is likely to generate hostile feelings among teachers even when it is in their own best interests. When teachers never express anger with the principal it may mean that he/she may not have made enough demands. The principal must not permit teacher hostility to reinforce self-doubt and withdraw from the real agenda. The supervision process described here involves a skillful integration of support (caring) for staff and demand (confrontation).

Chapter 11

CONCLUDING COMMENTS

This book was designed to serve as a resource for school principals and supervisors attempting to cope with the complex job of providing leadership in today's schools. The stresses on educators are increasing significantly while the available resources are shrinking. Schools are expected to do more with less and principals are held responsible for ensuring that they do just that.

Many of the problems faced by schools will persist until our society backs up its commitment to education with real resources. Until that time, principals and teachers must try to influence aspects of instruction and school culture which may improve learning opportunities for children. Improving teaching through supportive supervision is one area for such effort. The development of a school culture which offers a community of staff support for each other is another. The school principal can have a leadership role in achieving these ends. This book has focused on some of the dynamics and skills which may be useful in the pursuit of these purposes.

As school principals attempt to implement these roles, it is important that they have access to their own sources of educational and social support. As one principal expressed it: "It is hard to keep giving, if you are not getting support yourself!" This source of support can come from peers and other administrators, as well as from one's own staff. We hope this book will serve that function as well.

BIBLIOGRAPHY

Acheson, K.A., & Gall, M.D. (1987). *Techniques In The Clinical Supervision Of Teachers.* New York: Longman.

Alfonso, R. J. (1986). *The Unseen Supervisor: Organization and Culture as Determinants of Teacher Behavior.* Paper presented at the Annual Meeting of the American Educational Research Association (67th): San Francisco, CA. April, 16–20.

Berliner, D.C. (1986). The Half-Full Glass: A Review of Research on Teaching, in P. Hosford (ed.), *Using What We Know About Teaching.* Alexandria, VA: Association for Supervision and Curriculum Development.

Blumberg, A. & Jonas, R.S. (1987). Permitting Access: Teachers Controlling Supervision. *Educational Leadership, 44,* 8, 58–62.

Borich, G.D. (1990). *Observation Skills for Effective Teaching.* Columbus, OH: Merrill.

Berman, P., & McLaughlin, M. (1975). *Federal Programs Supporting Educational Change. Vol. IV, The Findings in Review.* Santa Monica, CA: Rand Corporation.

Brandt, R.S. (1987). On Coaching Teachers: A Conversation With Bruce Joyce. *Educational Leadership. 44,* 8, 12–17.

Brown, J.S., Collins, A., & Duguid, P. (1989). Debating the Situation: A Rejoinder to Palincsar and Wineburg. *Educational Researcher, 19,* 4, 10–12.

Carkhuff, R.R. (1969). *Helping and Human Relations: A Primer for Lay and Professional Helpers.* Vol. 1, *Selection and Training.* New York: Holt, Rinehart, and Winston.

Elmore, R.F. (1987). Reform and the Culture of Authority in Schools. *Educational Administration Quarterly, 23,* 4, 60–78.

Flanders, N.A. (1970). *Analyzing Teaching Behaviors.* Reading, MA: Addison-Wesley.

Floden, R.E. (1988). Instructional Leadership at the District Level. *Educational Administration Quarterly, 24,* 2, 96–124.

Fullan, M. (1982). *The Meaning of Educational Change.* New York: Teachers College Press.

Gattiker, U.E. (1990). *Technology Management in Organizations.* Newbury Park, CA: Sage.

Giandomenico, L.L., & Wolfe, M. (1988). Acknowledging Effective Teaching: A Key To Professional Growth. *SAANYS Journal,* Fall, 33–36.

Glickman, C.D. & Gordon, S.P. (1987). Clarifying Developmental Supervision. *Educational Leadership, 44,* 8, 64–68.

Goodlad, J., & Klein, M. (1970). *Behind the Classroom Door.* Worthington, OH: Charles A. Jones.

Gronn, P.C. (1983). Talk as Work: The Accomplishment of School Administration. *Administrative Science Quarterly, 28,* 1–21.

Haller, E.J. & Strike, K.A. (1986). *An Introduction To Educational Administration.* New York: Longman.

Hodgkinson, C. (1978). *Toward A Philosophy of Administration* Oxford, England: Basil Blackwell.

Hollander, E.P. (1961). Emergent Leadership and Social Influence, In L. Petrullo and B. Bass (eds.), *Leadership and Interpersonal Behavior.* New York: Holt, Rinehart, and Winston.

Hoy, W.K., & Forsyth, P.B. (1986). *Effective Supervision.* New York: Random House.

Huff, S., Lake, D., & Schaalman, M. (1982). *Principal Differences: Excellence in School Leadership and Management.* Boston, MA: McBer.

Hunter, M. (1984). Knowing, Teaching, and Supervising, in P. Hosford (ed.) *Using What We Know About Teaching.* Alexandria, VA: Association for Supervision and Curriculum Development.

June, D., Wenger, H., & Guzzetti, (1987). Personalizing Instructional Supervision Systems. *Educational Leadership,* 44, 8, 51–56.

Joyce, B.R., Hersh, R.H., & McKibbin, M. (1983). *The Structure of School Improvement.* New York: Longman.

Joyce, B.R., & Showers, B. (1982). The Coaching of Teaching. *Educational Leadership,* 40, 4–10.

Kadushin, A. (1976). *Supervision in Social Work.* New York: Columbia University Press.

Lewin, K. (1952). Field Theory in Social Science, In Dorwin Cartwright (ed.), *Frontiers in Group Dynamics.* New York: Harper and Row, 221–233.

Locke, E.A. (1979). The Supervisor as Motivator: His Influence on Employee Performance and Satisfaction, In R. Steers and L. Porter (eds.), *Motivation and Work Behavior.* New York: Mc Graw Hill.

Lortie, D. (1975). *School Teacher: A Sociological Study.* Chicago, IL, University of Chicago Press.

Maeroff, G.I. (1988). A Blueprint for Empowering Teachers. *Phi Delta Kappan,* 69, 7, 472–477.

Manasse, A. L. (1985). Improving Conditions for Principal Effectiveness: Policy Implications of Research. *Elementary School Journal,* 85, 439–463.

Maslow, A. (1954). *Motivation and Personality.* New York: Harper.

Natriello, G. (1983). *Evaluation Frequency, Teacher Influence, and the Internalization of Evaluation Processes.* Eugene, OR: Univ. of Oregon, College of Education.

Ornstein, A.C. & Levine, D.V. (1990). School Effectiveness and Reform: Guidelines for Action. *Clearing House,* 64, 115–118.

Rogers, C. (1961). *On Becoming a Person.* Boston, MA: Houghton Mifflin.

Ross, J.A. (1980). The Influence of the Principal on the Curriculum Decisions of Teachers. *Journal of Curriculum Studies.* 12, 219–230.

Sarason, S. (1971). *The Culture of the School and the Problem of Change.* Boston, MA, Allyn and Bacon.

Schein, E. (1968). *Process Consultation: Its Role in Organizational Development.* Reading, MA: Addison Wesley.

Schwartz, W. (1969). Private Troubles and Public Issues: One Social Work Job or Two. *The Social Welfare Forum,* New York: Columbia University Press, 22–43.

Schwartz, W. (1971). *The Practice of Group Work.* New York: Columbia University Press.

Shulman, L. (1991). *Interactional Social Work Practice: Toward an Empirical Theory.* Itasca, IL: F.E. Peacock.

Shulman, L. (1982). *The Skills of Supervision and Staff Management.* Itasca, IL: F.E. Peacock.

Shulman, L.S. (1983). Autonomy and Obligation: The Remote Control of Teaching, In L.S. Shulman and G. Sykes (eds.), *Handbook of Teaching and Policy.* New York: Longman.

Singh, J.V. (1990). *Organizational Evolution: New Directions.* Newbury Park, CA: Sage.

Webster, L. (1989). *The Real World of Administration: Reflections of First and Second Year Principals.* Educational Resources Information Center, Nov., 1–10.

Weick, K.E. (1976). Educational Organizations as Loosely Coupled Systems. *Administrative Science Quarterly,* 21, 1–19.

INDEX

155